THE POLITICAL PHILOSOPHY
OF BURKE

THE
POLITICAL PHILOSOPHY
OF BURKE

BY

JOHN MAC CUNN

NEW YORK
RUSSELL & RUSSELL · INC
1965

FIRST PUBLISHED IN 1913
REISSUED, 1965, BY RUSSELL & RUSSELL, INC.
BY ARRANGEMENT WITH EDWARD ARNOLD, LONDON
L.C. CATALOG CARD NO: 65-18817
PRINTED IN THE UNITED STATES OF AMERICA

CONTENTS

POLITICAL PHILOSOPHY
OF BURKE

CHAPTER I

THEORIES AND THEORISTS

THERE is a passage in Burke's writings in which he says that he does not vilify theory,[1] and the remark is truer than he knew. But it does not alter the fact that, in the whole range of our literature, there is no decrier of theories and theorists comparable to him. Sometimes he despises them ; sometimes he fears them ; always, or almost always, he appears to hate them. In a large proportion of his political writings there is a point at which, despite his deep-seated rationality, he drops argument and betakes himself to missiles. ' Refining speculatists,' ' smugglers of adulterated metaphysics,' ' atheistical fathers,' ' metaphysical knights of the sorrowful countenance,' ' political aeronauts '—these may suffice as fragments from the commination service. Or shall we add this, as sum of the whole matter : ' They are modern philosophers, which when you say of them you express everything that is ignoble,

[1] Speech in May 1782.

savage and hard-hearted.' Small wonder that he should declare that the propensity of the people to resort to theories is ' one sure symptom of an ill-conducted state.' [1]

This is remarkable. But it is not so remarkable as the fact that it is to this denouncer of theories, this vilipender of theorists, that the world has turned, and never in vain, not only for the oracles of practical wisdom, but for that large reasoning discourse upon the nature of society, and man's place in it as a political and religious animal, which makes it impossible to withhold from its exponent the designation of thinker, theorist, and philosopher. This is, in truth, the paradox of Burke's position as a political thinker. Constrained by the force of circumstances, not less than by personal proclivity, to turn from the theoretic to the practical life, he carried into affairs a reasoning imagination which had been fed and nurtured on wider pastures than those where politicians browse in happy unconsciousness of their limitations. He had dipped into philosophies ; it is evident, though the record of his intellectual debts is meagre and obscure, that, not to mention lesser names, he had studied Aristotle, Locke, and Montesquieu ; and he even appears, in early days, to have contemplated the tough task of refuting Hume. The *Philosophical Inquiry into the Origin of our Ideas of the Sublime and*

---

[1] Letter to the Sheriffs of Bristol.

Beautiful exists to show that he was not averse to an excursion of his own into æsthetic theory. And every speech, pamphlet, or treatise which he gave to the world is proof of the range of his reading, and not least in history and politics. Above all, he had thought profoundly, and argued himself with all comers into deep-seated convictions. The result was that, when he became a Whig politician, he was already far more. A mere politician he could not be. When he encountered a political problem it was not in him to deal with it in ordinary fashion, and to be content to cut knots with the blunt hatchet of common sense. ' He went on refining,' as Goldsmith said. And to good purpose. For the inherent rationality and penetrative insight of his mind were not to be denied. Hardly could a policy, a bill, an amendment, an administrative act come before him which he did not press back to principles with a thoroughness which raised it far above the levels of ordinary politics into the upper air of political thought. No politician, either in ancient or in modern times, has had so irrepressible a faculty of lifting even the passing incidents of the political hour into the region of great ideas. A rival candidate dies suddenly in the course of an election contest : ' the melancholy event of yesterday,' so runs Burke's comment, '. . . has feelingly told us what shadows we are, and what shadows we pursue.' An enemy attacks his well-earned pension, and

evokes that *Letter to a Noble Lord* (1776) which
Lord Morley has called the best repartee in the
English language ; as indeed it is, not only because
it goes home to the quick, but because it smothers
the spitefulness of the assailant in a flood of eloquence and wisdom. Similarly, and in intensified degree, when he handles the larger issues of
politics : he goes to meet them as a statesman, but
he never leaves them till he has enriched their discussion by the insight and reflection of the thinker.
For however he makes haste to disclaim acting
upon theory, this does not prevent him from theorising upon his actions. In truth, he theorised upon
them with such habitual persistence that no one
can rise from a perusal of his writings without feeling
that he has been led on to what falls little or at all
short of a political philosophy. A theorising politician is of course not the same as a political theorist,
but he is on the highroad to becoming one.

Yet this paradox (as we have called it) of Burke's
position is not so acute as might at first sight appear.
For it quickly becomes manifest that what he means,
in his diatribes, by a ' modern philosopher ' is precisely what a modern philosopher is not, if one may
be allowed to generalise from some of the best of
that diversified species. The theorists, the ' modern
philosophers ' Burke had in view, were the apostles
of abstract rights who had become, as he thought,
the victims of their own abstractions, and were so

fanatically in love with their own notions of man's 'natural' rights that they had quite forgotten man's nature and experience. In short, the word 'theorist' or 'philosopher' suggested to him the type of one-ideaed abstract thinker who is almost as much the abhorrence of some modern philosophers as of Burke himself.

For, thanks above all to Hegel, but also to writers as diverse as Coleridge, Comte, Macaulay, and John Stuart Mill, we have come to see that not only the theory of abstract rights, but all abstract political theories of a like kind are open to attack upon more sides than one. From the one side comes the reminder that abstract thought can never really wed fact, and is therefore doomed either to futility or fanaticism, if it does not come to terms with the force of circumstances. And from another side, not necessarily hostile to abstractions, we have the insistence that an abstract theory, even if it be granted that, within its own abstract province, it is the truth and nothing but the truth, is not the whole truth ; nor ever can be, till it is at once completed and corrected by equally legitimate abstractions, which along with it divide the many sided complex domain of concrete social fact. In the first of these two cases, abstract theory simply is confronted with the empirical facts of life and history ; in the second, it is bidden to accept its modest place as but one of many aspects which the rich and complex tissue of experience may offer to the dissecting knife of social analysis. Nor is anything more characteristic of modern philosophers than to insist upon one or other, or both, of these requirements. For philosophy has, for the most part, ceased to seek for reality in a region behind and beyond experience : it is more concerned to discuss and define what ' experience ' is. And one of the first fruits of this scrutiny is the disclosure of the fact that experience is much too complex and many sided to be understood either by any one-sided abstract method or by any purely observational method, and indeed demands, if justice is to be done to it, that analysis and abstraction should be freely pushed in many directions. For never can the concrete reality of things be understood till it has thus been exhaustively resolved into its constitutive forces, tendencies, and conditions.

Hence it turns out that, in his assaults upon theory and theorists, Burke renders theory a twofold service.

On the one hand, he is never weary of confronting abstractions with concrete facts. He is oftenest quoted as the prophet of ' circumstances.' ' I never placed your solid interests upon speculative grounds,' he said to his constituents. ' I must see the men, I must see the things,' he elsewhere cries. ' I never govern myself, no rational man ever did govern himself by abstractions and universals . . . : he who does not take circumstances into consideration is not erroneous, but stark mad—*dat operam ut cum ratione insaniat*—he is metaphysically mad.' [1] One more sentence (it has been quoted a thousand times) may clinch the point : ' Circumstances (which with some gentlemen pass for nothing) give in reality to every political principle its distinguishing colour and discriminating effect.' [2]

Yet this, even this, is not Burke's greatest service to theory. For it is a service greater still, and philosophically far more significant, that as he added speech to speech, and pamphlet to pamphlet, there grew under his hands a conception of civil society so rich, so comprehensive, so coherent, that it must stand, so long as English literature is read, as a touchstone of all abstract theories which, by failing to do justice to the complexity of the social system, fall into the pitfall, so perilous to abstract thinkers, of losing sight of the concrete whole in preoccupation with the limited, fragmentary, abstract part, aspect, or element. To see human life, no less than Nature, as a whole—this is of the essence of the philosophical spirit. It is also the spirit of Burke.

Nor are these the only services that this decrier of theories renders to theory. For, in the very force and fervour of his invective against ' modern philosophers,' he himself lights upon a principle of immense philosophical significance—none other than the old Aristotelian doctrine that the subject-matter

[1] Speech, May 11, 1792.   [2] *Reflections on the Revolution.*

of politics is by its very nature such as to baffle all attempts to reach results of scientific universality and exactness. No statements in all his writings are more emphatic than those upon this point. ' Nothing universal,' he roundly asserts, ' can be rationally affirmed on any moral or any political subject ' ; [1] and the sweeping generalisation is but one of many similar passages : ' No lines can be laid down for civil or political wisdom. They are a matter incapable of exact definition.' [2] ' Aristotle,' he remarks elsewhere, ' the great master of reasoning, cautions us, and with great weight and propriety, against this species of delusive geometrical accuracy in moral arguments, as the most fallacious of all sophistries.' [3]

It is manifest at a glance that this involves conclusions of nothing less than the first importance. It draws the distinction, Aristotelian in its emphasis, between the mathematical sciences and political science. It commits itself to the assertion that universal laws, strictly so-called, are in the nature of things unattainable in the latter. It avers, in short (with Aristotle), that a *science* of politics is impossible. Clearly, therefore, this sworn foe of theory has reached a theory of first-rate theoretical significance.

And all this, it may be added, is doubly valuable because Burke's assault upon abstract theory and

[1] *Appeal from the New to the Old Whigs.*
[2] *Thoughts on the Cause of the Present Discontents.*
[3] Speech on Conciliation with America.

abstract theorists cannot be said to have been historically victorious. For though it gave a blow to the doctrine of the ' rights of man,' against which it was directly levelled, a blow from which that memorable dogma never again quite lifted up its head, it did not prevent abstract theory from springing to life again in some of its most abstract forms. The first quarter of the nineteenth century was to see the Benthamite theory of government expounded, by the uncompromising logic of James Mill, in what Burke would have called ' all the nakedness and solitude of metaphysical abstraction.' Almost simultaneously, Ricardo, one of the most abstract minds the world has ever seen, developed a political economy with a disregard of ' circumstances ' so pronounced as to have led one critic [1] to brand his work as ' an intellectual imposture.' And not less unfalteringly, John Austin, building on Hobbes and Bentham, gave the world, the English world at any rate, that juristic doctrine of Sovereignty which has always, and rightly, been regarded as one of the most thoroughgoing specimens of the abstract and analytic, as contrasted with the historical method. And Austin, needless to say, was long, and even to our own day is, a commanding figure in English jurisprudence.

Nor is this vitality of abstraction and abstract method to be lamented. It has a permanent value.

[1] Toynbee in his *Industrial Revolution*.

For it may well suggest, and it has suggested, that the right path for the political philosopher lies, not in a repudiation of abstraction—for this would be the abandonment of analysis—but rather in pressing abstraction in many directions, and thereby preparing the way for a comprehensive social synthesis in which competing—though by no means irreconcilable—abstractions may find at once their completion and corrective.

None the less Burke's influence remained. It is at any rate in harmony with the drift of his teaching that Macaulay, his enthusiastic eulogist—'our greatest mind since Milton,' he calls him—urged, with all the resources of his rhetoric, the claims of a 'Baconian' inductive method, in that controversy without quarter in which he withstood James Mill and the Benthamite theory of government to the face. So when Comte, in his enthusiasm for a concrete social science, waged a war of extermination against abstract political economy. So not least, when J. S. Mill was constrained to acknowledge that, in that duel between his father and Macaulay over the Benthamite theory of government, James Mill was wrong, and even to assert that a science of government—that doctrine so dear to his father's heart—was impossible.[1] And so also at a later time, when Sir Henry Maine, deeply dipped in the history of institutions, and keenly

[1] Cf. *Logic*, Bk. vi. c. ix.

alive to the qualifications which Austinian 'sovereignty' must experience in the eyes of all students
of early law and custom, declared that Austinian
identification of law with force, and of sovereignty
with the fiat of a political superior, would need for
its verification the discovery of an absolute despot
with a disturbed brain.[1] Nor is it less in the spirit
of Burke that nineteenth-century sociology should
have so frankly embraced the historical method.
For whether by 'historical method' we mean simply
the inductive study of institutions as they present
themselves in history, or, more precisely and
properly, the genetic study of institutions as they
pass through phases of historical development, the
historical point of view is substantially that of
Burke when he turned away, with many a gibe and
sarcasm, from abstraction and all its ways, and
declared that his was the better foundation—the
foundation laid in the actual concrete, verifiable
experience of men and nations. It is no doubt
difficult to judge how far these writers of the nineteenth century draw upon Burke. For Burke's
thought, not being avowedly theoretical, has never
won adequate acknowledgment from avowed theorists. But, be this as it may, few contributions
to method are more valuable than Burke's whole
handling of the 'philosophers' of abstraction. The
results of his handling of the theorists are far wider

[1] *Early History of Institutions.*

than its aim. Its aim was to overthrow pestilent
fanatics who were recklessly rushing to reform
and revolution with 'rights of man' and suchlike
watchwords, or catchwords, on their lips : its results were to open the eyes of every reader of his
works, from the *American Speeches* onwards, to the
nature of political fact, to the difficulties of social
investigation, and to the limitations that dog the
steps of analysis and generalisation the moment
they turn from the mathematical or physical world
to try to frame a science of society.

This was a service of the first magnitude. The
century that was about to begin when Burke died
(1797) was to see science freely extending its interest
from Nature to man. And nothing could be more
fortunate than that, on the threshold of this adventure, it should have its eyes opened to the nature
of the new order of facts with which it had to deal.
This was what Burke was pre-eminently fitted to
do. He was steeped in politics. He knew what
political fact was by lifelong contact with it. He
'saw the men : he saw the things.' He realised
the complexity and ever-shifting combinations of
the world of affairs. He understood the force of
circumstances. He looked at society as a whole.
And in these ways, by the irony of fate, in denouncing 'modern philosophers,' he furnished in his
speeches and writings one of the best of all intro-
ductions to modern social philosophy.

All the more so because, despite the constant appeal to facts and the gospel of ' circumstances,' Burke's attitude is by no means purely empirical. Though he argues from experience, and is never weary of claiming that his generalisations are ' the arguments of kingdoms and nations,' it is not to be supposed that he approaches experience with that complete repudiation of all presuppositions which has sometimes been extolled as the glory of the Baconian inductive method. On the contrary, no one can go far into his pages without becoming aware that his thought is profoundly influenced by convictions which he takes for granted. Some of them are psychological, and some are metaphysical. That man is ' a religious animal ' ; that he is likewise a ' political animal ' ; that all ordinary men are creatures in whom feeling, habit, even prejudice are apt to be stronger than reason ; that they act on motives relative to their interests far more than on theories ; that they are much quicker to feel grievances than to find remedies—these are amongst the principles of his psychology. He does not prove them. He does not feel himself called upon to prove them. He had made up his mind on most, or all, of them long before he entered politics. But he constantly appeals to them. It is not enough for him therefore that a political generalisation should be drawn from history : he seldom rests till he has added that it is confirmed, or, it may be, shaken, by all that we know of human nature. To phrase the matter in the language of the schools, he constantly tests political inductions by a psychology that is none the less firm because it is forthcoming only in fragments scattered throughout his pages.

Similarly, and in greater measure, with the presuppositions that are metaphysical. For it would be nothing less than a fatal misconception to write down Burke as a purely inductive thinker. Even he who runs as he reads must soon discover that, in the background of all his political thought, there lie large assumptions which profoundly influence the conclusions which he draws. That God willed the state, that He willed likewise the nation of man, and that the whole course of a nation's life is 'the known march of the ordinary providence of God'[1]—these, and much else that depends on them, are fundamental articles of his political creed. These high doctrines, needless to say, are never proved. They are held as a faith. But, then, they are held with a tenacity so great, and urged with a reiteration so insistent, that they not only colour, but saturate all he has to say about the nature and the sanctions of the social order. Few points indeed are of greater interest to the readers of Burke than the relation between these sweeping theological principles and that inductive

[1] *Regicide Peace*, Letter II. : 'The rules of prudence which are formed upon the known march,' etc.

appeal to history and fact which is, in the eyes of many of his students, his distinctive characteristic.

This will be clearer in the sequel. For the present it is enough to suggest that though students of philosophy may naturally enough prefer to study political philosophers by habit and repute, it may be doubted if they ever study that subject at greater advantage than when they have the opportunity of tracing the process whereby a great mind, versed in affairs and steeped in practicality, is so instinct with the philosophic spirit as to be forced far across the frontier of practical politics into the larger world of political theory. Such, at any rate, is the opportunity which, in unique degree, is to be found in the life and writings of this great theorising assailant of theorists. The writings are, naturally, the main concern ; but it may prepare the way to glance at some not irrelevant aspects of the life.

CHAPTER II

FROM KIN TO KIND

IT is well known to readers of biography that Burke was a self-made man. When enemies jeered at him as 'an Irish adventurer,' this was but the malevolent version of Prior's tribute to him as ' the first person who, under so many disadvantages, attained to consequence in Parliament and in the country by his own unaided talents.' As he said himself, when driven to *apologia pro vita sua* by that ungenerous attack on his well-won pension to which reference has already been made, he had to show his passport and prove his quality at every step of his laborious career : ' I had no arts but manly arts. On them have I stood, and, please God, in spite of the Duke of Bedford and the Earl of Lauderdale, to the last gasp will I stand.' [1]

In a struggle like this, any man might be forgiven some forgetfulness—the forgetfulness not of want of heart, but the more excusable forgetfulness of want of thought and want of time. Yet the only thing Burke seemed to forget, as his best

[1] *Letter to a Noble Lord.*

biographer [1] justly remarks, was his own interests.
Certainly there are few more satisfying chapters in
biography than the record of his fidelity to the private
ties and obligations of life.   And not to kindred only.
It is characteristic that the last lines he wrote were
words of consolation to the daughter of Shackleton,
the friend of his boyhood.   Nor did absorption in
public affairs prevent him from turning aside to
rescue the genius of Crabbe from the last extremes
of poverty, to render unwearying thankless service
to the erratic painter Barry, to befriend the friend-
less Armenian adventurer Emin, whom one day he
found wandering in the Park.   When he kept house
in Beaconsfield in later years, suffering peasants and
French exiles were equally the objects of his care
or hospitality.   And it need hardly be said that, of
all the friendships of men of letters, none can surpass
his with Johnson, Reynolds, Goldsmith, Garrick,
and the rest who have made the Turk's Head
as memorable as the Mermaid.   ' Ah ! ' exclaims
Thackeray, in words easy to re-echo, ' I would have
liked a night at the Turk's Head, even though bad
news had arrived from the colonies, and Doctor
Johnson was growling against the rebels ; to have
sat with him and Goldy ; and to have heard
Burke, the finest talker in the world ; and to

[1] Lord Morley : ' There is much good material in the Lives by
Prior and MacKnight, but readers in search of living portraiture
must turn to *Burke* in " English Men of Letters," and to *Burke :
A Historical Study.*'

have had Garrick flashing in with a story from his theatre.' [1]

Such things, of course, needed no theories to prompt them. They were instincts of the heart. But they are none the less illustrative of certain settled convictions, again and again avowed, which Burke held as to the right relation between the private and the public affections. For when Burke called Rousseau ' a lover of his kind ; a hater of his kindred,' the taunt was no mere bitter epigram. It conveyed, and was meant to convey, the suggestion that the man who hates his kindred is not likely to love his kind. For, in the natural history of the wider human ties, as Burke understood it, growth does not begin all at once at the circumference. From kin to kind is the true order of development. Men must learn experimentally what ties are, and what duties are in the home and the friendly circle, if they are to develop sympathies worth the giving to the neighbourhood or the nation. ' No cold relation is a zealous citizen '— so runs his formula. ' To be attached to the subdivision, to love the little platoon we belong to,' is the first step, and the reality of the wider sympathies is suspect if it be not built on fidelity to the lesser relationships that lie at our feet.

It is not the whole truth. It cannot be, if there be any truth at all in the ascetic creed that ' the

[1] *The Four Georges.*

forlorn hope in the cause of mankind must have no
narrower ties to divide the allegiance.'[1] But this
is no part of the gospel of Burke. Nor is it the
general law of the genesis of public interests. Nor-
mally the charities of life begin at home, not, of
course, because the claims of family and friendship
are more imperative than the service of city or
nation, but for the better reason that the civic
virtues, unless one is to suppose that they fall like
manna from heaven, spring naturally from the
kindly soil of ordinary human intercourse.

We find the same principle, though on a larger
stage, when we turn to Burke's attitude to political
party.

It need not be said that Burke was a party politician. From his entrance into the House in 1765,
it is well known that he threw in his lot with the
Rockingham Whigs, and that, for the next five-and-
twenty years ' night by night in the forlorn hope
of constant minorities,' laboured, as few politicians
have ever laboured, to build up the party in face
of the dogged hostility and corrupt influence of
George III. and the various ministries which, after
1766, the Whigs strove in vain for many a year to
oust from power. ' In the way they call party I
worship the constitution of your fathers '—this was
his boast. And, in the spirit of the words, this

[1] Robertson of Brighton, *Sermon on ' Marriage and Celibacy.'*

' John Wesley of politics ' not only gave to political
party as an institution a vitality which since his
day it has never lost, but wrote in the *Thoughts on
the Present Discontents* the best plea for party in
our own or in any language.

It was, of course, not his theory of party that
made him thus a party man. Men do not join
parties to illustrate theories. He became a Whig
because he held certain political principles—he had
formed them, he declares, before he had so much as
set foot in St. Stephen's,—and because the Whig
party, or the section of it that followed Rockingham,
seemed to him the best instrument for making these
principles effective. All his life he was, as he often
said, a practical politician, a combatant not a spec-
tator, whose prime business it was to promote good
measures and resist bad ones. Nor had he any love,
as we have seen, for politicians who acted on theories.
They filled him with distrust, derision, and denunciation. Yet none the less he had his justification of
party. For it was an article of his creed that if a
politician means to serve his country, the path to
all effective service lies through loyalty to party.
All the world knows how Goldsmith once, in *Retalia-
tion*, satirised his friend for giving up to party what
was meant for mankind. But the taunt was in
reality a tribute. For mankind was not defrauded,
nor ever could be, by Burke's becoming a Whig;
because, in his creed at any rate, it was in and

through party that political work for mankind
could best be done. No one ever felt this more
convincedly than Burke. No one ever looked with
a deeper distrust upon the politician without party.
No one ever more vehemently denounced the loose
allegiance that, with the shibboleth ' not men but
measures,' rides off, usually to impotence (' unpitied
sacrifice in a contemptible struggle ' are his words)
upon personal ideals, policies, fanaticisms, or
crotchets, and with a light heart casts to the winds
' the practised friendships and experimented fidelity '
which bind comrade to comrade in great public
causes. No one was ever more convinced that
strong party was one of the prime securities of
liberty.

And yet, as every reader of history knows, though
Burke lived for his party, he did not die in it. The
French Revolution came, and, in face of the issues,
not to be evaded, which it raised, latent divergencies
sprang to light and the Whig party fell into ruins.
Needless to tell again that familiar tale of inevitable
rupture, embittered division, and renounced friendship ; the point that alone concerns us is its explanation. Many have said that Burke was inconsistent,
or worse. Bentham and Buckle have imperilled
their own reputation for sanity by pronouncing
him mad. ' It is at any rate ' (to use words of his
own), ' the madness of the wise, which is better than
the sobriety of fools.' But the truth is that the one

imputation is as false, though not so absurd, as the other. The more temperate, and to the student of Burke's writings the convincing explanation is simply that, much as Burke loved his party, he loved his country more. Instead of being stigmatised for infidelity to party, he stands to be lauded for the courage of convictions that relegated party ties to their proper and subordinate place.

For when any man throws in his lot with a political party as an invaluable instrument of action, he need not, and, indeed, if he be open-minded he cannot, pledge himself to take his political convictions from it. The world will not blame him, perhaps, if he attach something more than their weight to the oracles of the party in which he finds himself, but his convictions, if they be more than echoes, will be fed from wider sources. Not all the springs of political wisdom rise in the land of Whig, or of Tory, or of Radical party, or even in all of them put together. Burke is a case in point. He did not take his convictions on trust either from ' new Whigs ' or ' Old Whigs,' even if he attached what some may regard as more than their due to the dicta of the latter.[1] He had a wider outlook. He had read widely and thought much. He had observed with the eye of the man of affairs ; and, partly by nature, partly by experience, he had gained the insight of genius. The result followed. His life and thought

[1] As *e.g.* in the *Appeal from the New to the Old Whigs.*

came to be dominated by a patriotism which in
fervour has never been surpassed, and in utterance
seldom equalled. 'I owe to this country my
labour, which is my all ; and I owe to it ten times
more industry, if ten times more I could exert.' [1]
There are avowals stronger still : ' Do me the
justice to believe that I never can prefer any fas-
tidious virtue (virtue still) to the unconquered
perseverance, to the affectionate patience of those
who watch day and night by the bedside of their
delirious country, who for their love to that dear
and venerable name bear all the disgusts and all
the buffets they receive from their frantic mother.' [2]

It is, however, only when we have some idea of
the object which evoked this unfaltering patriotism
that we can understand its influence upon Burke's
attitude to party. For that object was a widely
different thing from the conventional and abstract
entity which ' nation ' or ' country ' too often
suggests to popular thought. It was a singularly
concrete, comprehensive, and well-compacted reality
which had emerged in the world of men by the
labours of many hands and many minds all working,
sometimes consciously and sometimes unconsciously,
under the ultimate direction of a ' Divine tactic.'
Therefore it was not to be identified with either
crown or aristocracy, or landed interest, or moneyed

[1] Speech on the Economical Reform.
[2] Letter to a Member of the National Assembly.

interest, or parliament, or electorate, or populace—
not with any of these singly, because with all of them
in richly integrated organic union. For if a nation
be indeed a ' partnership,' in the sense that Burke
read into that word,[1] then must it stand altogether,
if it stand at all, and move altogether if it move at
all. One member or element must not usurp upon
another, or arrogate to itself more than its appropriate function in the subtly and harmoniously knit
system of the body politic ; any more than, in the
body physiological, this organ or that organ, this
function or that function, can ignore its necessary
co-operation with other organs and other functions
which along with it constitute the living unity of the
whole. Nothing, as we shall abundantly see, is
more constantly reiterated in Burke's pages than
this idea of balance, equipoise, harmony, organic
unity. Nor is it only to the political constitution
in the narrower sense that he applies these and suchlike categories ; it is to the constitution of civil
society as a whole.

This was Burke's idea of a nation. This was
what he saw actually realised in the England of his
day. This was the object that enkindled his patriotic devotion. It may be, as has often enough
been said, that in seeing it he was looking, in part
at any rate, at his fancy's own creation. But even
if this be true, it would only prove that he loved

[1] Cf. p. 59.

his country because of what he conceived it ought to be, as well as for what he held it to be in fact.

It was upon this conception of his country that, from first to last, Burke took his stand. In his earlier career he saw authority and royal influence usurping our popular institutions, and so he withstood the influence of the Crown in the name of liberty. These were the days when he sided with Wilkes and the Middlesex electorate against the House of Commons ; when he urged repeal of the restrictions that strangled Irish commerce ; when he denounced the fatuity of American policy ; when he pled with a convincing persuasiveness against the disabilities of the Irish Catholics ; and when, all along, he was in the front rank of the Whig battle against old royal prerogative in the new dress of corrupt Georgian influence. The scene changed, and when the French Revolution had come, he saw in Radical ideals and popular movements a menace to the constitution from another side ; and so he withstood them too. It was then he broke with Fox, and denounced Paine, and ridiculed Price, and poured contempt on Rousseau, and dropped bitter words about the ' swinish multitude,' and won the plaudits of old enemies by ' diffusing the Terror.' It is open to critics to think that he was wrong in one or other or all of these points. ' The King's friends ' thought him in the wrong in the earlier years ; the ' new Whigs ' thought him equally

in the wrong after the Revolution. But at any rate
he was consistent, if fidelity to principles be consistency. Lord Morley has here, with his usual
felicity, put the whole question in a nutshell when
he says that Burke changed his front, but never
changed his ground.[1] For it was precisely because
he held his *ground* so tenaciously that, in face of
changed circumstances and new problems, he felt
constrained to change his *front* so decisively that he
was fated to worship the constitution of his fathers,
not in the way men call party, but in the way they
call patriotism, even by rupture of party ties. It is
not the least of his legacies. In all party ridden
countries strong parties run a risk of creating narrow
men. It is good to be reminded that even the
greatest party is after all a part, and that fidelity
to party ties, however necessary, however honourable,
is dearly bought if the price be loss of the larger
outlook and the patriotic spirit. It is not to be
lamented that, by the fortunate irony of history,
the greatest of our apologists of the party system
should have been also a monument of its limitations.

Political sympathies and ideas, however, are not
bounded by the nation. They certainly are not now,
when the cosmopolitan idea appears conspicuously
enough, not only in religion and ethics, but in practical philanthropy, international law, finance, com-

[1] *Burke* in 'English Men of Letters,' p. 169.

merce, and industry. Nor were they then, when
revolutionary France was offering her ' fraternity '
to all peoples ; when ' the ambassador of the Human
Race,' mountebank though he was, had been received
in all seriousness by the French Assembly ; when
Paine, in writings that ran to one hundred thousand
copies, was foreseeing an European republic with
man free of the whole ; [1] and when it was the claim
and the boast of Whigs as well as Radicals in England
that they were no whit worse patriots because their
sympathies overleaped the frontiers of the nation
and went out freely, not only to America and France,
but to all struggles for freedom where there were
wrongs to right, or rights to win.

Now it is not to be supposed that Burke was
devoid of cosmopolitan ideas and sympathies. We
meet in his pages many a word and phrase—' mankind,' ' the species,' ' the race,' ' the great primæval
contract of eternal society,' ' the great mysterious
incorporation of the human race,' all of which
suggest that his thought moved in a large political
orbit. Nothing can be more striking than the ease
and familiarity with which his mind ranges in the
wide sphere of international politics, in his handling
alike of the American crisis and the French Revolution.[2] Even when, in the *Letters on a Regicide
Peace*, he was preaching war to the death against

[1] *Rights of Man*, p. 70.
[2] See *e.g.* the *Thoughts on French Affairs*.

the 'regicide republic,' it was in anything but an insular spirit. On the contrary, he always had a lofty conception of the part which England was called upon to play in the politics of the world. ' I was convinced,' he said in 1794, ' that war was the only chance of saving Europe, and England as included in Europe, from a truly frightful revolution ' ; and it is a comment on the words that his death was felt as a calamity for Europe. And this was not merely policy : it was principle. The Machiavellian spirit was alien to his nature ; he always believed in a higher law, ' an order that holds all things fixed in their place,' to which nations as well as individuals are eternally subject. Human laws were, in the last resort, only ' declaratory '—declaratory of ' an original justice ' that is above and beyond all legislators.[1] So, too, he argues that there is a ' law of civil vicinity ' which ' is as true of nations as of individuals,' and which ' has bestowed on the grand vicinage of Europe, a duty to know, and a right to prevent, any capital innovation which may amount to the erection of a dangerous nuisance.' [2] Nor will it be forgotten, one may hope, either in the East or the West, that he gave the years of his prime to the championing of the wrongs of the millions of India against what he regarded as the flagitious rapacity of their rulers, in days when the duties of England to her

[1] *Tracts on the Popery Laws.*　　[2] *Regicide Peace*, Letter i.

distant dependency were but faintly realised. In
all these ways he was without doubt cosmopolitan
enough.

Nevertheless, it was not from this wider outlook
that he drew the real nerve and passion of his
political inspiration. However wide his range of
idea, he was, all his life through, profoundly under
the influence of the spirit of locality. ' The locality
of the affections ' was one of the points of his faith.
' Do you know,' he once wrote, thinking of his own
early home, ' I had rather rest in the corner of a
country churchyard than in the tomb of all the
Capulets.' The same spirit impelled him, as we
have seen, to seek the seedplot of the wider interests
in private ties, and to graft something of the fidelities
of friendship upon political association. Similarly
with the sentiments that come of the natural human
intercourse of neighbourhood. None of his many
points against the revolutionists of Paris is urged
with more conviction than his warning against the
wanton sacrifice of the social bonds that come of
locality, which he saw in the subjection of a newly
subdivided France to the centralised despotism of
Paris. ' It is boasted that the geometrical policy
has been adopted, that all local ideas should be
sunk, and that the people should be no longer
Gascons, Picards, Bretons, Normans, but Frenchmen, with one country, one heart, and one assembly.
But, instead of being all Frenchmen, the greater

likelihood is that the inhabitants of that region
will shortly have no country.' [1]

The same trend of thought carried him with it,
in a wider application, when he encountered the
cosmopolitanism that menaced the tie of patriotism.
And this was what he was convinced the cosmopolitanism of the Revolutionists and their English
sympathisers did. To his eyes it had the fatal
defect of being reared on the negation of patriotism,
and sometimes even of all those lesser ties out of
which a real patriotism is woven. 'Benevolence
to the whole species, and want of feeling for every
individual with whom the professors come in
contact '—this is the indictment that comes in
his invective on Rousseau,[2] that 'ferocious, low-
minded, hard-hearted father, of fine general feelings.'
'Their humanity,' he says of them in general,
'is at the horizon, and like the horizon it ever
recedes before them.' 'On that day' (it was the
day when the Opposition denounced the war with
France as unjust), 'I fear there was an end of
that narrow scheme of relations called our country,
with all its pride, its prejudices, and its partial
affections. All the little quiet rivulets that watered
an humble, a contracted, but not an unfruitful field
are to be lost in the waste expanse and boundless
barren ocean of the homicide philanthropy of

---

[1] *Reflections on the Revolution.*
[2] Letter to a Member of the National Assembly.

France.'[1] For to Burke, as later to Mazzini, the only cosmopolitanism that could be genuine and of worth was that which, to borrow the formula of Coleridge, comes by antecedence of patriotism ; with the result that ' humanity,' ' the species,' ' the race,' and all similar conceptions, were forthwith to be numbered amongst the abstractions he detested, if they did not gather up into themselves the rich and varied content of the habitual ties and tried allegiances which can alone give substance to the idea and service of the nation. Hence his quarrel with French ' fraternity,' which had become in his eyes no better than a catchword, pretentious, empty, unsatisfying, and powerful only as a deadly solvent of patriotism.

The surprising feature here is undoubtedly the acuteness of Burke's apprehensions. Even now, despite the indubitable advances which the cosmopolitan spirit has made in the course of the nineteenth century, it can hardly be maintained that cosmopolitanism *by negation of patriotism* is anything approaching to an imminent danger. The danger that threatens comes rather of the growth of that spirit of nationality which is certainly one of the most masterful forces of the political world of the present day—so masterful indeed that cosmopolitan ideas and sentiments seem strikingly inadequate to repress it. For however true it be that the spirit

[1] *Regicide Peace*, Letter III.

of locality, in many of its lesser old-world aspects, has perished, or is fast perishing, before the solvents of wider ideas and larger interests ; and however manifest it is that many of the traditional local attachments and sentiments, so dear to Burke's heart, are going down before the activities of central-ised legislation, these signs of the times cannot be taken as proof that local patriotism, especially in the supreme form of national allegiance, is vanishing or likely to vanish from the world.   On the contrary, the spirit of locality appears to be assuming new and fruitful forms under the reorganisation of the modern state.   When popularly elected parish and district and county councils do their work, there is not likely to be a diminution of local interests. When towns and cities vie with each other in the stimulating rivalries of municipal enterprise, there is room enough for civic spirit and provincial pride in the place of a man's birth or adoption.   When large sections of our country are, in season and out of season, clamouring for more control of their own affairs, the spirit of locality is certainly alive.   Nor are these new ties necessarily weaker because they are so much more deliberate and self-conscious than the older traditional attachments which they are superseding.   And least of all is this the case when the object of local patriotism is the nation.   Few facts indeed seem more incontrovertible in our day than that the citizens of all nations, however open

to cosmopolitan ideas and influences, are becoming
aware, as never before, that the national heritage
is the national responsibility. How indeed could it
be otherwise, when the fact is brought home to
them, in the burdens of armaments, and in intensified national rivalries, bursting out at times into
sanguinary wars, which the international situation
has developed ? Small wonder that it should be
dawning upon the minds of even the least militant
of citizens that, in the absence of any power higher
than the nation to enforce the dictates of a cosmopolitan justice, it still rests with themselves and their
fellow-countrymen, and with no one else, to conserve, defend, and transmit their national heritage
inviolate to their posterity. What other conclusion
can be drawn, so long as every nation of the world
appears to act upon the settled conviction that its
own continued existence, and the fulfilment of its
own destinies, are essential to civilisation ? Those
who adventure on the darkly veiled paths of political
prophecy may descry the advent of another dispensation. They may dream with Cobden of the
coming of a time when the barriers between nations
will be broken down by commerce ; or with some
of the Socialists, of a day when the common cause
of Labour all the world over will swamp the rival
interests that divide peoples ; or with Mazzini, of
the realisation of an international system in which
the several nations, more intensely national than

ever, will hold their organised strength as a trust
for mankind. Be it so. Yet the point remains that,
if such a transformation of Europe is to come, it
does not yet at any rate seem to be coming through
that cosmopolitanism by negation of patriotism
which Burke so dreaded and denounced.

It is needful to dwell on these considerations
because they carry in them a criticism of Burke.
They convict him of a mistaken, and even an
alarmist, emphasis. All his insight, knowledge,
and wisdom did not save him, in his horror of
French fraternity, from over-rating the strength
and dangers of the cosmopolitanism of his day.
His fears for his country, which were the other
side of his passion of patriotism, drove him to hurl
against the cosmopolitans a whole arsenal of
flouts, sarcasms, and invectives, which may all too
readily be appropriated by the Machiavellian
apostles of blood and iron who recognise no wider
interests than the greeds, and no higher law
than the needs, of the self-centred and self-seeking
nation.

Not that Burke was without his provocations
either. It unfortunately happens that, in the ranks
of cosmopolitanism, there are individuals who
seem unable to indulge their humanitarian sympathies without setting themselves in aggressive
hostility to the patriotic spirit, and even denouncing
it as a ' bias,' a superstition, or a crime. Nor is it

a sufficient plea for such that their attitude may be
prompted by lofty motives, and by the entirely
true perception that patriotism, like every other
great human passion, may go wrong. For at no
time is a nation more in need of the loyalty of a
citizen than when he believes it to have gone wrong.
It is precisely then that he is called upon, not to
indulge in general declamations against patriotism,
which is the strength and security of every people,
but rather ' to sit ' with Burke ' by the bedside of
his delirious country,' and to spare no patriotic
effort to restore it to what he believes to be a saner
and a juster mind. It is pardonable to indulge
the hope that it is possible to hold fast to cosmopolitan ideas and sentiments, and yet to turn away,
with Burke and Mazzini, from the cosmopolitanism
of apostate patriotism. Nor is it to be forgotten
that there were facts before Burke's eyes which go
far to explain the virulence of his antipathies here.
Apart from the excesses of the ' homicide philanthropy ' of the revolutionists, ' in the groves of whose
Academy,' as he savagely said, ' at the end of every
vista you see nothing but the gallows,' there were
conspicuous figures before his eyes, in whom the
cosmopolitan confession of faith was suspect because
it seemed to come so easily. When Tom Paine
capped Franklin's ' Where is liberty, there is my
country,' by the amended version, ' Where is *not*
liberty, there is mine,' the sentiment was noble.

It is worthy of a political crusader. Who does not wish to re-echo it from his heart ? But it has a less impressive force, when we remember that it came from a political soldier-of-fortune whose allegiance to any country in particular was so loose that, in his shallow-rooted, nomadic life, he played, not without self-glorification, the rôle of citizen of three. This was what Burke distrusted and abhorred. It was in sharpest contradiction, as must now be evident, to all he believed and felt about the growth of the social and political affections. That no cold relation can be a zealous citizen, that the locality of the affections enriches life, that personal friendship can be grafted upon political comradeship, that ' the combined and mutually reflected charities ' of ' our state, our hearths, our sepulchres, and our altars ' must be inseparably interwoven in the national life [1]—these were amongst his most passionate convictions. And, true to the same spirit, he held the faith that a single-minded and unfaltering patriotism must needs be the normal path to the service of mankind. But as the idea of mankind, the species, the race, was still, in his day as in ours, vague, undefined, and imperfectly realised, it is not to be wondered at that, to a mind like his, intent upon actualities and impatient of abstractions, it was still in the idea of the nation, say rather in the realised idea of the British people,

[1] *Reflections.*

that he found the central source of his political inspiration.

This, however, will be more evident when we pass from this brief sketch of his general attitude to the substance of his teaching as to what a nation is.[1]

[1] P. 50.

CHAPTER III

ONE of the most interesting points about a man of
affairs is the way in which he approaches and solves
his practical problems. Is it by the reasoning that
links together means and ends ; or is it by the swift
intuitive decision that seems to reason not at all ;
or is it, in whole or in part, by appeal to authority,
be it the authority of traditions or persons or institutions ; or is it rather by some combination of
all three methods ?

Now this is a matter on which Burke is explicit.
He has left us in no possible uncertainty as to what
he deems the paramount virtue of the man of
affairs. ' Prudence,' he declares, ' is not only the
first in rank of the virtues, political and moral, but
she is the director, the regulator, the standard of
them all.' [1] This being so, the question that emerges
is obvious : What is this ' prudence ' that is thus so
unhesitatingly promoted to the primacy ?

Clearly, to begin with, it is to be sharply distinguished from the characteristic virtue of the theorist.
The theorist thinks first and last of truth and

---

[1] *Appeal from the New to the Old Whigs.*

error : the man of affairs is concerned with good
and evil. The theorist has but one thing before
him at a time ; his problem is simplified by the
familiar, necessary artifice of abstraction, more or
less rigorously applied : the statesman is confronted
by all the baffling complexity of concrete situations
in which considerations of good and evil, advantage
and disadvantage, meet and cross and intermingle
in ever varying proportions and combinations.
Unlike the abstract thinker, he must see, or try to
see, everything and neglect nothing. Hence the
peculiar, and sometimes crushing, difficulty of the
statesman's task. Moving, as he must, in the
troubled, perplexing, and shifting medium of concrete circumstances, and thrust on by the imperious
urgency of crises that brook no delay, he cannot
indulge in that suspense of judgment, which is one
of the virtues of the theorist, nor pause to work out
his problems theoretically. Time forbids it. Nor
can he have recourse to thinkers or theorists who
will solve his problems for him. Easy and light
would be the burden of the statesman if, in the
urgent hour of his perplexity, he could turn to some
political adviser, some casuist in politics, to find his
problems theoretically anticipated, and their solutions already made. But no such thing is possible.
The nature of political fact precludes it. In the
complex interaction of human wills and social
forces and endlessly varying circumstances, the

problems, if they be serious, are such as no theoretical acuteness can have foreseen, and no theoretical foresight solved by anticipation. And just for that reason there is no course open to the man of affairs but to take upon his own shoulders the burden of facing his problems for himself, and solving them to the best of his ability by his own ' prudence.' For if the tangled knots of politics are to be dealt with, it will not be by the philosopher who unravels them at his leisure : sooner or later, and often enough sooner rather than later, they must be cut by the statesman who is fortunate enough to possess the practical wisdom, the ' prudence,' to grasp and weigh the circumstances of the situation, and the nerve to decide what the day or the hour or the moment requires to be done. Small wonder therefore if Burke sets such store on ' prudence ' as to dignify it as the mother of all the virtues. For his glorification of prudence, like Aristotle's laudation of φρόνησις,[1] is but the inevitable complement of that doctrine of ' circumstances ' which, as we have already seen,[2] led him roundly to declare that no lines could be theoretically laid down for civil and political wisdom.[3]

And yet it must not be supposed that, because ' prudence ' does not come to its decisions by theory,

[1] *Ethics*, Bk. VI.   [2] P. 7.
[3] For Burke's contrast between the theorist and the statesman, see Speech, May 11, 1792, and Speech for Shortening the Duration of Parliaments (date doubtful).

it is therefore purely intuitive. For however sharp
the contrast between the statesman and the theorist
or 'professor,' as Burke sometimes calls him, it does
not imply that ' prudence ' can dispense with
principles and the application of principles to facts.
And it is of especial importance to take note of this,
not only because the practical man (as he calls
himself) is notoriously apt, in contempt for theory,
to pin his faith to instinctive common sense, but
because Burke himself has, often enough, been
taxed with substituting prejudice for judgment and
drawing his inferences with his passions rather
than his understanding. Nothing could be further
from the mark. For the ' prudence ' of Burke's
panegyric is neither a sense nor an instinct. It is
apt to be mistaken for such because its decisions
are often so swift as to seem intuitive. But as
Burke himself remarks, in speaking of judgments
of taste,[1] this celerity of its operation is no proof
that it needs a distinct faculty to account for it.
For whatever intuitive element it may, and indeed
must, include, seeing that no man can in matters
of detail go on deliberating for ever, and however
passions and even prejudices may colour its valuations, it is fundamentally a virtue of the reason.
He has himself said so. ' I have ever abhorred,' so
runs a declaration of his later years, ' since the first

[1] Introduction to *Inquiry into our Ideas of the Sublime and
Beautiful.*

dawn of my understanding to this its obscure twilight, all the operations of opinion, fancy, inclination, and will in the affairs of government, where only a sovereign reason, paramount to all forms of legislation and administration, should dictate.' [1]

Not that it is difficult to find passages which, on a superficial perusal, might seem to have a very different ring.   One occurs in the ' Speech on American Taxation ': ' If you apprehend that on a concession you shall be pushed by metaphysical process to the extreme lines, and argued out of your whole authority, my advice is this : when you have recovered your old, your strong, your tenable position, then face about—stop short—do nothing more—reason not at all—oppose the ancient policy and practice of the empire, as a rampart against the speculations of innovators on both sides of the question ; and you will stand on great, manly, and sure ground.'   The words are strong, but it would be a serious mistake to take them as if meant to carry a depreciation of the reason declared to be sovereign and paramount. They are levelled only against that bastard reason which all his life he detested—the reason of the one-ideaed fanatic of ' the hocus-pocus of abstraction,' who, having seized an abstract principle, insists upon pushing it to the extreme of logical illation, in all ' the nakedness of metaphysical abstraction,' and in defiance of the inevitable friction of concrete

[1] *Letter to a Noble Lord.*

circumstances.   Nor is it the man who in this fashion
pushes principles to extremes (as if he were reasoning in a vacuum) who thereby establishes his claim
to rationality.   Rationality in politics at any rate,
whatever it may be in the abstract sciences, is more
convincingly evidenced by holding fast to principles
in presence of the stubborn difficulties of actual
fact, which it is much easier to ignore than to
rationalise.   This is the kind of reason at any rate
that Burke had in view from the first dawn of his
understanding to its obscure twilight.   Nor did he
the less believe it to be ' paramount ' because he
set himself so copiously to denounce the abstract
theorists and metaphysicians of politics.

It follows that the man of affairs whose sovereign
virtue is ' prudence,' who is also the statesman after
Burke's own heart, is likewise the man of principles,
and far removed from the type who blindly trusts
his instincts, even when he calls his instincts his
conscience.   'Without the light and guide of sound,
well-understood principles,' so runs one of many
similar statements, which may be taken as conclusive, ' all reasonings on politics, as in everything
else, would be only a confused jumble of particular
facts and details, without the means of drawing
out any sort of theoretical or practical conclusion.' [1]
Two things, therefore, Burke would have us distin-

[1] Speech, May 11, 1792 ; and cf. his denunciations of ' the
profane herd of vulgar and mechanical politicians ' who disbelieve
in principles.

guish. The one, which he distrusts, is to act upon
theory ; the other, which he commends, to act
upon principles. The first of these can never be
other than the way of fanatics or madmen : the
second is the path of sanity and statesmanship.
These two things, it may be granted, are not easy
to sunder. For when principles are not only definite
but coherent, as the principles held by Burke will
be found to be, it is obvious that the line between
acting on a theory and acting on principles becomes
difficult to draw. And it is doubtless the perception of this that brings this denouncer of theories to
declare at times (though not often) that he has no
aversion to theories. ' I do not vilify theory and
speculation,' he says, ' no, because that would be
to vilify reason itself. *Neque decipitur ratio, neque
decipit unquam.*' [1] And though this was said (in
1782) before the theories of the ' French philosophers ' had unsealed the vials of his invective, he
could repeat the same thing ten years later : ' I
do not put abstract ideas wholly out of any question, because I well know that, under that name, I
should dismiss principles.' [2] We might wish that
he had pushed these admissions further. These
pages indeed will fail of their object if they do not
make it evident that all his life through, Burke's
political judgments were rooted in theory to an
extent which he seems imperfectly to have realised.

[1] Speech, May 7, 1782.   [2] Speech, May 11, 1792.

So much so that it is impossible to suppress the wish
that a mind so essentially philosophical had done
more to gather into systematic shape the mass of
singularly coherent principles which readers are
left to glean from his pages for themselves. But to
ask for this would be to ask that Burke should be
other than he was. By profession he was a statesman, not a theorist. And when, with the practi-
calities of day and hour before him, he grasped a
principle, his first instinct was, not to weave it into
a system of thought, but to use it and apply it to
circumstances. The result followed. Forthwith the
principle, ceasing to be an abstract thought, was
utilised as a rule and instrument of ' prudence,'
and as such became subject to all the inevitable
abatements and qualifications which must always
come when thought weds fact, and theory meets
practice.

It will be the object of succeeding chapters to
extricate these principles, and to exhibit them in
their coherency. But meanwhile we may, with
advantage, limit ourselves to one particular group,
the interest of which lies in the fact that they are
so frankly utilitarian. Almost indeed we might
fancy at times, when we encounter them, that
somehow we had strayed from the pages of Burke
into those of Bentham. Thus we read that ' it is
the direct office of wisdom to look to the consequences
of the acts we do ; if it be not this, it is worth

nothing.' [1]   If this be not utilitarian, what is ?   Yet
it is not more utilitarian than many other utterances equally explicit : ' The object of the State
is (so far as may be) the happiness of the whole.
. . . The happiness or misery of mankind, estimated by their feelings and sentiments, and not by
any theories of their rights, is, and ought to be, the
standard for the conduct of legislators towards the
people.' [2]

Nor can there be a doubt that these were principles on which Burke himself consistently acted.
Dazzled by his rhetoric and the passion of his utterance, the world has come to think of him too much
as a man of emotions and intuitions ; and critics
of his own day, and since, have dealt with him too
often as if he were an inflammable political partisan
and combatant, betrayed by political and even
personal passions into all manner of emotional
exaggerations and prejudiced judgments.   ' He
loved to exaggerate every thing '; says Lord
Holland, ' when exasperated by the slightest opposition, even on accidental topics of conversation, he
always pushed his principles, his opinions, and even
his impressions of the moment to the extreme.' [3]
So he did.   Restraint, either in feeling or utterance,
was not in his temperament.   But the correction
to this, and to all similar verdicts, lies in words of

---

[1] Speech, May 11, 1792.   [2] *Ibid.*
[3] Lord Holland's *Memoirs.*

his own : ' Vehement passion does not always
indicate an infirm judgment.' For though the
passion, not to say the fury, of Burke's utterance
is not to be denied—who would dream of denying
it who recalls the pages of the *Reflections* or the
Regicide Peace ?—the inference is not that, because
Burke said many vehement things, he was no wise
man, but rather that no so profoundly wise man
ever said so many vehement things. Few pages
are richer than his in luminous sentences that have
the serene light of wisdom on them. ' I am most
afraid of the weakest reasonings, because they discover the strongest passions.' ' He censures God
who quarrels with the imperfections of men.' ' The
tyranny of a multitude is a multiplied tyranny.'
' Kings will be tyrants from policy when subjects
are rebels from principle.' ' Those who attempt
to level never equalise.' ' Equal neglect is not
impartial kindness.' ' They who always labour can
have no sound judgment.' ' Wisdom is not the
most severe corrector of folly.' ' But calamity is
unhappily the usual reason for reflection ; and the
pride of men will not often suffer reason to have
any scope until it can be no longer of any service '—
these may serve as bricks from the temple. Similarly with innumerable sustained passages too
lengthy for quotation. For, in truth, when due
allowance is made for the fact that all his life long
Burke was on his own avowal a passionate com-

batant in the stormy strifes of politics, the distinctive mark of his genius is its sanity. Even in
those pieces where the whirlwind of his passion and
invective is at its height, his wisdom and rationality
are never far off. This is apparent even in the
Regicide Peace, for, though these fiery pages ransack
the English language to find vituperative missiles—
robbers, assassins, cannibals—it is in them we find
towards the end of the Third Letter—a tribute to
the old Greek virtue of moderation. ' Our physical
well-being, our moral worth, our social happiness,
our political tranquillity, all depend on that control
of all our appetites and passions, which the ancients
designed by the cardinal virtue of temperance.' [1]
And it is in keeping with the words that the Letter
ends on the note of ' responsibility.' Nor was it
without good reason, though the immoderation of
his words often obscures the fact, that the virtues
to which perhaps above all others he laid claim,
were consistency and sobriety of judgment. ' In
reality,' he wrote to his intimate friend Laurence,
when the hand of death was already on him (the
topic was the prosecution of Hastings), ' you know
that I am no enthusiast, but according to the
powers that God has given me, a sober and reflecting man.' [2] ' Please God,' he said on another
occasion, when describing his own procedure, ' I
will walk with caution, whenever I am not able

[1] *Regicide Peace*, Letter III.   [2] Feb. 10, 1797.

clearly to see my way before me.' [1] 'It may be allowed,' so runs still another dictum, 'to the temperament of the statesman to catch his ultimate object with an intuitive glance ; but his movements towards it ought to be deliberate.' [2] It was this deliberateness, this sobriety, this rationality which constrained him, throughout his career, and even in utmost stress and bitterness of party passions, to turn to principles as the necessary rules and standard of the ' prudence ' of his panegyric, and not least to keep unwaveringly before him ' the happiness of the whole ' as the end of all political work. And this utilitarian phrase finds reinforcement in the variant (one of many) that ' those on whose account all just authority exists ' are ' the people to be governed.' [3]

It would, however, be a misnomer to call Burke utilitarian—at any rate till we construe ' happiness of the whole ' or ' happiness of the people ' in the light of his conception of what a people is. For it will quickly appear that this is vastly different from anything that is to be found in the Radical gospel of Bentham and the Benthamites.

[1] Letter on the Duration of Parliaments.   [2] *Reflections.*
[3] Letter to the Sheriffs of Bristol.

CHAPTER IV

WHAT IS A PEOPLE ?

FROM the beginning of his political career Burke seems to have already formed a definite conception of what a people is, which, if it changed at all, changed only, as the years went on, in the direction of maturity and clearness. The best expression of it is to be found in some pages of the *Appeal from the New to the Old Whigs*, which are amongst the most luminous in the whole of his writings. The passage is much too lengthy for quotation ; but this is the less necessary because the keynote of the whole may be said to be struck in the three words, ' discipline of nature.' ' When great multitudes act together, under that discipline of nature, I recognise the PEOPLE.' [1]

What then is this ' discipline of nature ' which thus avails to gather men together and give them the unity of a people, or, to use the phrase that meets us oftenest in Burke's pages, of a civil society ?

The answer is that it is that long and gradual process of historical development, divinely guided, as Burke believed, through which the many hands

[1] *Appeal.*

and many minds of successive generations slowly
bring a society out of the rude and undisciplined
state, when as yet a ' people ' cannot be said to
exist, into that state of organisation in which the
varied elements of a corporate life, throne, aristocracy, church, judiciary, parliament, electorate,
non-electorate, professions, trades, science, art,
morality, manners—all find their appropriate place
and function.   In a sense this corporate life implies
a compact or agreement.   Burke says it does.   He
speaks of ' the original compact or agreement which
gives its corporate form and capacity to a State.' [1]
He even says that the idea of a people is ' wholly
artificial and made, like all other legal fictions, by
common agreement.' [2]   But these and other terms
and phrases which he freely borrows from the
philosophy of the eighteenth century must never
be taken to mean that he thought, as Hobbes or
Rousseau thought (or at any rate say), that a
' people ' was called into being once for all by an
explicit act of contract in some far-off imaginary
past.   If compact there be, it is a compact of a
kind that is tacitly rather than explicitly, gradually
rather than by any single transaction, made, as the
growth of corporate life advances from generation
to generation.   Much as he makes of ' the original
contract ' in arguing about 1688 against the New
Whigs, it is the contract ' *implied and expressed in*

[1] *Appeal.*   [2] *Ibid.*

the constitution of this country,' not the contract as a single transaction.[1] No idea, indeed, is more repugnant to Burke than the notion that any mere multitude of men, whether savage or civilised, should at a given time, and by their own explicit choice, fabricate a state by contract. It filled him, he says, and it is evident without his saying it, ' with disgust and horror.' ' Alas ! ' he exclaims, ' they little know how many a weary step is to be taken before they can form themselves into a mass which has a truly politic personality.' [2]   For it is by ' the discipline of nature,' as it operates through the centuries, and not by the abrupt initiatives of parties to an explicit contract, that peoples and states are fashioned and perpetuated.

This was the conception of a ' people ' that was central in Burke's thought from the beginning, and it carries in it further conclusions of far-reaching significance.

One of these is that a ' people ' is a highly complex unity.   For when Burke speaks of the ' discipline *of nature,*' the word ' nature ' suggests to him nothing whatever of the associations of artless, primitive simplicity, social or political, that gathered round the fancied state of nature in the minds of the disciples of Rousseau.   That vision of a simplified social life, a life that had escaped the inconveniences and limitations of savagery, and yet had

[1] *Appeal.*   [2] *Ibid.*

not fallen victim to the artificialities, vices, and
'chains' of advanced civilisation, had no charms
at all for Burke.   One of his earliest literary adventures, *The Vindication of Natural Society*, was an
elaborate satire designed to unmask its hollowness
by a *reductio ad absurdum*.   The picture repelled
him.   He regarded it as a proof that its admirers
were lacking in the barest rudiments of political
knowledge and wisdom.   'When I hear of simplicity of contrivance aimed at and boasted of
in any new political constitutions, I am at no loss to
decide that the artificers are grossly ignorant of their
trade or totally negligent of their duty.' [1] Two
pregnant aphorisms justify this condemnation.   The
one is that 'art is man's nature,' [2] the other that
'nature is never more truly herself than in her
grandest forms.   The Apollo of Belvedere is as
much in nature as any clown in the rustic revels
of Teniers.' [3] For it is only necessary to piece
these together to develop the conclusion that we
shall never understand what the 'discipline of
nature' can achieve till we turn away from the
'savage and incoherent' life of primitive man to
the complex, richly differentiated, and highly organised structure of a civilised society.   To Burke the
belauded state of nature of the Rousseauites is little,
if at all, better than the 'city of pigs' satirised by

[1] *Reflections.*   [2] *Appeal.*
[3] *Regicide Peace*, Letter III.

Plato in his *Republic*, or than the 'solitary, poor, nasty, brutish, and short' life of pre-social man as delineated in the trenchant pages of Hobbes. His conception of 'nature' and the 'natural' is in its essence Greek to the core. It is the Aristotelian conception of the organised 'natural' municipal State read into the life of the modern nation.

Nor can it be doubted that the truth here rests with Aristotle and Burke. It has become a commonplace of evolution that, the more fully evolved societies become, they are, by the very laws of social growth, immeasurably more richly integrated than the more primitive forms which have sometimes carried captive the imagination of apostles of the simple life. And though there is nothing in this, as many an ugly social fact too clearly shows, to prevent the growth of societies, like other forms of growth, from running to rankness and disease, so that luxurious, corrupt, distempered, ill-conducted States need the remorseless knife of revolutionary surgery ; yet the laws of social development are not thereby abrogated. For even when revolution, though it were ten times repeated, has done its drastic work, the result is never a permanently simplified society. On the contrary, the irrepressible vitality of the social system, purified as by fire, reasserts itself, and the State finds itself once more advancing in the path of growth which leads from the simple to the complex, from loose aggregation to intimate integration of parts and members, and which stretches onwards along that line of advance whereby the unity of a people is intensified by the illimitable triumphs of organised specialisation in its myriad forms.   To try to reverse this process, to re-trace this path—what is this but to fly in the face of all that the history of institutions has to tell us of the growth of States ?   Grant that there is a place for simplification.   Grant that there is a time for reform.   The man is not to be envied who cannot, with Bentham, execrate the complication, confusion, and unintelligibility of bad laws ; or who cannot with Paine anathematise the barriers between man and man and ' the wilderness of turnpike gates which have been set up between man and his Maker ' by bad governments ; or who cannot with Wordsworth lament the materialism and artificiality which choke the truer life.   Yet neither is it to be supposed that these moods and movements are endings.   They are really new beginnings.   So far from being the journey's end, they are but places of regeneration where the spirit of man renews its powers for fresh effort in its endless forward march.   Never can they bring those who face the facts of history to wish seriously to set themselves to fight against the very laws of life.   ' As well rock the grown man in the cradle of the infant,' as Burke has it.   In a word, they cannot justify rebellion against ' the discipline of nature.'

This leads to a further point. For it must be already evident that Burke's conception of a people as 'under the discipline of nature' involves a complete divergence from that identification of a people with the aggregate of its units, or a 'greatest number' of them, which, in the generation that followed, was the distinctive mark of Bentham and the Benthamites. In the light of Burke's teaching all such arithmetical categories are seen in a moment to be thin and inadequate to the facts. A mere mass of men, still less a mere majority of a mass of men, is not a people. ' It is said that 24,000,000 ought to prevail over 200,000. True, if the constitution of a kingdom is a problem of arithmetic.' So Burke wrote,[1] when denying the claims of a majority by count of heads to work its will in politics ; and the words are but one of many illustrations of his decisive rejection of mathematical categories as inadequate to social fact. For on his view, as must now be evident, a people cannot be said to exist at all, save when the mere multitude or mass of men has been organised by the discipline of nature in the long course of actual historical evolution. Apart from this, a people dissolves into an incoherent, disbanded mob which is the sheer negation of a civil society ; for, as it seems to be the law of life that the social organism, like other organisms, advances towards organisation ; and as it is through organisation that

[1] *Reflections.*

it gets its work done, it cannot divest itself of this
its character as a developed society, without thereby
ceasing to be a people in the true sense of the word.
The happiness of the whole, in other words, can
never be the happiness of a people or nation or civil
society or commonwealth (call it by what name we
will) unless it be, as it was to Burke, as to Plato, the
happiness of an organic whole.

For Burke, as must now be evident, had firmly
grasped our latter-day conception of society. The
eighteenth century had called society a contract ;
the nineteenth has rebaptized it as an organism.
And there can be no doubt which of these categories
Burke prefers. Not that he refuses to call society
a contract. He often does. For, as already said,
he is far from having divested himself of the terminology of his age. But, even in the passages in
which he does this, two points emerge quite clearly.
The one is that he is little, if at all, interested in the
student's question, whether society had its actual
historical origin in a contract. The contractual
theory becomes interesting to him, as a practical
thinker, only when and because it was made the
ground of the claim that the members of an existing State, and even a majority of their number, by
the exercise of that free individual choice which the
notion of a contract suggests, could overturn the
existing constitution and set up a new one in its
place—a claim which he always withstood to the

uttermost. And the second point is that, though this implacable antagonism to the author of the *Contrat Social* and all his following did not prevent him from using their terms—'contract,' ' pact,' ' convention,' and suchlike—it led him to regard society as a contract or convention of a peculiar kind. For the ' contract ' he has in mind always involves those slowly evolved, habitual, intimate, living ties between the members and classes of the body politic which are so clearly *not* the product of any explicit act of contract between man and man, or class and class that they have driven our sociologists to lift society above the categories of law and plunge it deep in the categories of biology. Nor is it too much to say that all the main implications which justify the currency of this now somewhat trite analogy are to be found in Burke's pages. Justly does Lord Morley (writing in 1879) conclude his illuminating estimate of Burke's life and writings [1] with the prophecy that Burke ' will be more frequently and more seriously referred to within the next twenty years than he has been within the whole of the last eighty.' It will be strange if it is otherwise in the century that has now begun, for though Burke's words are often those of the eighteenth century, his thought is that of the nineteenth. Far more so than the thought, not only of Hobbes, Locke, and Rousseau who moved in the atmosphere of contract, but of Bentham,

[1] *Burke* in ' English Men of Letters.'

Cobden, and even Mill, who, though they had left contract behind, had not yet advanced to the conception of organism. 'Society,' so runs the classical confession of his faith on this point, 'society is indeed a contract. Subordinate contracts for objects of mere occasional interest may be dissolved at pleasure—but the State ought not to be considered as nothing better than a partnership agreement in a trade of pepper and coffee, calico or tobacco, or some other such low concern, to be taken up for a little temporary interest, and to be dissolved by the fancy of the parties. It is to be looked on with other reverence ; because it is not a partnership in things subservient only to the gross animal existence of a temporary and perishable nature. It is a partnership in all science ; a partnership in all art ; a partnership in every virtue, and in all perfection. As the ends of such a partnership cannot be obtained in many generations, it becomes a partnership not only between those who are living, but between those who are living, those who are dead, and those who are to be born. Each contract of each particular State is but a clause in the great primæval contract of eternal society, linking the lower with the higher natures, connecting the visible and invisible world, according to a fixed compact sanctioned by the inviolable oath which holds all physical and all moral natures each in their appointed place. This law is not subject to the will of those who by an obligation

above them, and infinitely superior, are bound to
submit their will to that law.' [1]

This passage is decisive. It parts Burke by a gulf
from both Rousseau and Bentham. For Contract
it, in effect, substitutes Growth : for Greatest Number it reads Social Organism. The categories of law
and arithmetic are dethroned, and the conceptions
of biology advanced to the supremacy.

Yet this supremacy is not unqualified ; and it is
to Burke's credit that he is awake to its limitations.
Not only did he see, and say, that the conception of
society as an organism was merely analogical ; he
recognised the precise point on which the analogy
is weak, and may readily, by its assimilation of
social to natural organisms, pass into a pernicious
dogmatism. For the writers, from Locke, and even
from Hobbes onwards, who invoked the contract,
were not without their reasons. They saw that a
political system, if it is to be justifiable, must rest,
in some sense, upon agreement, choice, or consent.
The real reason why they make so much of their
fancied contract is not that they thought they were
offering the world a chapter in the history of origins,
in which, indeed, they had but a feeble interest, but
that the conception enabled them to find a place
for human will and private judgment in the constitution of society. Even Hobbes, apologist of despotism though he be, recognises individual will in

[1] *Reflections.*

the contractual act by which the contracting parties enslave themselves for ever. Nor are these claims for individual will gratuitous or irrational. For however appropriate it may be, because closer to the facts, to call society an organism, it is admittedly one of the dangers of the conception that, in thus closely assimilating the social to the natural order, it is prone to do less than justice to the part that is played by individual wills in all social and political causation. 'Constitutions,' we are told, in well-worn words, 'grow and are not made.' The positive statement is true, but it would be better to leave out the 'not.' Constitutions grow and *are* made. For whatever be the process of growth, it must find room for that initiative and energy of individual wills to which it is difficult to find a sufficiently close analogy in the growth of plant or animal. However helpful biological categories may be, they must not be suffered to obscure the undoubted fact that, from the clan or the family onwards, and most of all in a civilised society, the wills of the units are capable of much.

This is what Burke sees, and his perception of it appears with much clearness in several passages, which are the more noteworthy because there is so much denunciation elsewhere in his writings of the radicals who were bold enough to claim that they could choose their own rulers, and frame a government for themselves. In one of these passages he is arguing against the theory that States have necessarily the same stages of infancy, manhood, and decrepitude as are found in the lives of the individuals who compose them. ' Parallels of this sort,' he proceeds, ' rather furnish similitudes to illustrate or to adorn than supply analogies from whence to reason. The objects which are attempted to be forced into an analogy are not found in the same classes of existence. Individuals are physical beings, subject to laws universal and invariable. The immediate cause acting in these laws may be obscure : the general results are subjects of certain calculation. But commonwealths are not physical but moral essences. They are artificial combinations ; and, in their proximate efficient cause, the arbitrary productions of the human mind. We are not yet acquainted with the laws which necessarily influence the stability of that kind of work made by that kind of agent.' [1]

The force of this is obvious. It makes three statements, each of the utmost importance : the *first*, that the ' similitude ' between the individual and the social organism does not by any means run upon all fours ; the *second*, that this is so because the ' things forced into an analogy are not found in the same classes of existence ' ; and the *third*, that the human mind is ' the proximate efficient cause ' in the construction and maintenance of the State.

[1] *Regicide Peace*, Letter i.

And to these we may add two corollaries, the first
from the immediate context and the other from an
earlier piece. *The one* is the fact, so suggestive of
the romance of politics, that, by intervention of
individual agency, many events occur, in the vicissitudes of States, as contrasted with the uniformity of
the physical world, so unexpected that they are
often set down to chance or divine interposition.
' The death of a man at a critical juncture, his
disgust, his retreat, his disgrace, have brought
innumerable calamities on a whole nation. A
common soldier, a child, a girl at the door of an inn,
have changed the face of fortune, and almost of
nature.' [1] *The other* corollary is practical, and words
can hardly be stronger in the protest they carry
against the political quietism which may all too
easily flow from the acceptance of the given social
system as if it were a part of the unalterable order
of nature. It is worth quoting at length : ' These
analogies between bodies natural and politic, though
they may sometimes illustrate arguments, furnish
no argument of themselves. They are but too often
used under the colour of a specious philosophy, to
find apologies for the despair of laziness and pusill-
animity, and to excuse the want of all manly efforts,
when the exigencies of our country call for them
more loudly. How often has public calamity been

---

[1] E. S. Payne, in his enlightening notes on the *Regicide Peace*,
identifies the soldier as Arnold of Winkelried, the child as
Hannibal, the girl as Joan of Arc.

arrested on the very brink of ruin by the seasonable energy of a single man. . . . I am as sure as I am of my being that one vigorous mind, without office, without situation, without public function, of any kind (at the time when the want of such a thing is felt), I say, one such man, confiding in the aid of God, and full of just reliance in his own fortitude, vigour, enterprise, and perseverance, would first draw to him some few like himself, and then that multitudes, hardly thought to be in existence, would appear and troop about him.' [1]   And it is in keeping with these sentences that one of his latest injunctions to his friends, when the sands of life were running, was ' Never succumb.'

But Burke went much further even than this. For where, one may well ask, is a belief in ' the proximate efficient causation ' of individual wills more forcibly affirmed than in the many hundred flaming pages in the *Reflections* and the *Regicide Peace*, in which he was diffusing the terror ?   For Burke diffused the terror because he felt it.   He was convinced that the radicals in England, like the revolutionists in France, had capacities for infinite mischief.   Miss Burney tells us, in words not easily forgotten, how, in his later years, he could not even speak of the Revolution without his face immediately assuming ' the expression of a man who is going to defend himself against murderers.'

[1] Letter to William Elliot.

Critics may call this panic, but, even if it were, it
sprang from the entirely deliberate conviction, again
and again repeated, that the Radicals of his day, if
not withstood to the face, had it in them not only
to wreck the constitution of England, but even to
destroy civilisation and usher in a new barbarism.
And his words of alarm and denunciation were
levelled against not only the outstanding leaders,
but the rank and file, the mob of Paris, who had
given so notable a demonstration of ' the proximate
efficient causation of the human mind ' by over-
turning, as it were in the twinkling of an eye, an
ancient, imposing, and (as men had thought) a
firmly rooted monarchy. ' It is asserted that this
Government ' (*i.e.* the Revolutionary Government)
' promises stability. God of His mercy forbid. If
it should, nothing upon earth besides itself can be
stable.' [1]

The result of all this is manifest. It makes it
evident that Burke's conception of a ' people ' has
two aspects, not easy to reconcile. On the one
hand, he has grasped the idea that society is an
organism—grasped it so firmly as to see and say
that the social system comes to maturity in obedience to laws of growth that are above and beyond
the competence of individual wills to alter.[2] And
when this aspect is to the front, one rises from his

[1] *Regicide Peace*, Letter IV. This letter was written before
the others.   [2] Cf. p. 59.

pages all but convinced that it is the whole political
duty of man to recognise the social system as if it
were part of the fixed order of nature, and to accept
his situation as a thing decreed for him and not
chosen by him. On the other hand, we meet the
conviction, no less firmly held, that the proximate
efficient causation of the human mind is so masterful a force, that human wills may even overturn
the constitution of the state and lay civilisation
in ruins.

Not that he leaves these two aspects apart and in
antagonism. He at least suggests a synthesis in
the pregnant principle that ' art is man's nature,'
and that there is therefore a large sense of ' nature '
and the ' natural ' wide enough to include human
agency. Even more important is the theistic
faith—of which we shall see more in the sequel—
which prompts the far-reaching principle that, as
man's nature and the State are alike the manifes-
tations of the Divine will, they must be presumed
to be harmoniously adapted each to the other.
Nor is there any principle in the whole of his writings
with which Burke is more in earnest than this.[1]

How far these principles avail to make his thought
self-consistent, and in particular how far they
reconcile his frank recognition of the efficient causation of the human mind in the making of the State,
with his undoubted anticipation of the latter-day

[1] See p. 84 et seq.

notion that society is an organism—this is a question
we shall be in a better position to answer when
we have seen something of the influence of his
conception of a 'people' upon his practical
conservatism.

CHAPTER V

(a) *The Impracticability of Radical Reform*

BURKE'S conservatism is not a conservatism of
sentiment, and still less of prejudice. It is the
conservatism of principles. And there are two
principles of wide generality on which it rests. *The
one* is the conviction that, by the very nature of a
civilised society as well as by the nature of man, all
radical reconstruction of a political system is, to
put the matter bluntly, simply a thing that cannot
be done, though, of course, it may be attempted :
the other, that, for the same reasons, reinforced by
the fact that man is a moral and religious, as well
as a political being, it is a thing which ought not to
be attempted. We may take these points in turn.

Turning to the first, it may be granted that it
is an arguable question whether the latter-day
conception of society as an organism tells more in
favour of conservatism or of radicalism. But there
can be no doubt as to its influence on Burke. In
his case, it is conservative to the core. For, from a
wide survey of life, he returned with a deep and

68

unalterable conviction that, whatever happiness be
within reach of a people—and he never lost sight
of the happiness of the people as the ultimate end—
this is only to be won slowly, and by making the
most of existing conditions which, so far as the
efforts of any single generation are concerned, are
in great measure inexorable. This seemed to him
to follow from that conception of a people which we
have just been examining. For a civilised society,
like all highly developed products, has come to be
so manifoldly differentiated in organs and functions,
and so cunningly integrated in the relation of its
parts, that the resulting whole is a miracle of organisation. Add to this that of the elements thus
unified—and in these elements fall to be included
not only institutions, but the ideas, sentiments,
and habits that gather round them—by far the
greater number, as indeed the very notion of organic
growth suggests, send their roots deep into the
past, and Burke's inference lies ready to hand. He
draws it at any rate without any hesitation. For
what is it but a monstrous and upstart usurpation
that any man or association of men should set
themselves up, at a given epoch of a nation's life,
to reconstruct *de novo* a product like this ? It is too
great, too complex, too intricately fashioned, too
firmly rooted in the persistent trend of historic
tendencies. Better, because saner, to accept it, in
essential features at any rate, as if it were part of the

order of nature, as in the higher sense of 'nature' it is, and to dispose our lives and frame our projects accordingly. For never, if Burke is to be believed, does the path to the happiness of men and nations lie through sweeping innovation; always it lies in doing justice to the past, in welcoming what it has achieved as 'an entailed inheritance,' and even in the hour of reform, when reform is needful as it sometimes is, in carrying it through in a spirit of gratitude and reverence towards existing institutions, which, as they certainly have not been made, are as certainly not to be remade, by the energies of any single generation of radical reformers, however ardent their passion for human happiness may be.

This is the secret of those passionate exhortations in which Burke adjures the reformer to approach the defects of his country as he would the wounds of a father, with pious awe and trembling solicitude; this that constrains him to require of the statesman a heart full of sensibility, a love and respect for his kind, and a fear of himself; this that prompts the avowal that he would rather distrust his judgment than condemn his species; this that inspires the faith that, though the individual may be foolish, the species is wise; this that evokes the declaration that if he cannot reform with equity he will not reform at all; this that impels him to affirm that all titles rest ultimately on prescription; this that brings him to invest even the machinery of an existing constitution with a sacro-sanctity it can never really possess ; and this, not least, that inflames him to eye all revolutionists, nay, even all radical reformers, with the contempt of the skilled mechanician when he sees the bungler meddling with the springs and balances of a delicate machine,[1] or, as we might more fitly say, with the indignation of the surgical expert when he sees the knife of the quack menacing the still more delicate organism of the human body. This is his ever-recurring refrain.   And, in the later days especially, when Revolution theory and Revolution excess had stirred him to the depths, it waxes so shrill and passionate as almost to drown the soberer mood in which he had sometimes paid his tribute to ' the great law of change,' and even recognised it as a condition of the conservation of society.[2]

Nor is this conservatism merely a general inference from the analogy of the organism, with all its suggestions of gradual, persistent growth and continuity. It has also definite and specific grounds, drawn more directly from his immense knowledge of men and affairs.   And amongst these two are salient.

(a) In the first place, he was convinced that the distance between any plan or programme of radical reform and its realisation was, by the very constitution of human nature, vast.   ' The little catechism of the *Rights of Man,*' to take the instance

[1] *Appeal.*   [2] Letter to Sir H. Langrishe.

that was most to the front, could be quickly got by
heart, and new constitutions rapidly enough ex-
cogitated by the resourceful arts of an Abbé Sieyes
and the pens of ready writers.   But it is simplicity
itself to fancy that from these, and suchlike things,
it can be other than a long and arduous road to the
engrafting of them upon the slowly won habits and
habitual sentiments and 'just prejudices' of an
organised people.   No thinker, indeed, has ever
grasped more firmly than Burke the fact that man's
habits and sentiments lag far behind his ideas ; and
that whilst ideas, theories, projects, declarations
may capture the imagination at a stroke, they can
be wrought into life only under inexorable limits of
time.   It is here that his psychology profoundly influences his politics.   Hence the frequent antithesis
in his pages between habits and sentiments without
ideas, and ideas without sentiments and habits, and
his avowed preference for the former.   'Politics
ought to be adjusted not to human reasonings but
to human nature.' [1]   Hence, too, his tenderness
towards what may appear to be no more than hoary
prejudices.   For it is largely of 'just prejudices'—
so he will have it—that the substance of men's duties
is made.   What else are we to make of the averment
that 'the moral sentiments' are 'so nearly connected with early prejudice as to be almost one and
the same thing.' [2]

[1] *Observations on a Late State of the Nation.*   [2] *Appeal.*

Not, of course, that he had any wish that politicians should part company with ideas. He had certainly ideas enough of his own, and we have already
seen his unstinted tribute to principles. But there is
always the per contra that, if men of affairs are not
to degenerate into vapouring theorists and ' political
aeronauts,' they must respect the nature of the
human material in which, as political craftsmen, they
have to work ; and, holding fast to ' prudence, the
mother of all the virtues,' recognise the force of circumstances with which, whether they like it or not,
they must needs reckon. This was a lesson he himself had early learnt. Once, in a sentence startling
enough—it was comparatively early in his career—
he told the House that ' he had taken his ideas of
liberty very low ; in order that they should stick to
him, and that he might stick to them, to the end of
his life.' [1] It was only his way of saying that he
took a sober view of what reform could do. And
this spirit grew upon him, as might be expected, in
direct proportion as reform began to pass into (what
seemed to him) revolution. We hear less, far less in
the later years, of the reforms that are the conservation of the state, and more of the innovations,
which are not reforms, of ' speculatists,' ' fanatics,'
' theorists,' and ' able architects of ruin.'

(b) To this we must add the further principle, and
there is none more consistently urged, that the

[1] *Appeal.*

practicability of any reform is to be measured, not merely with reference to the particular grievances and abuses it is meant to extinguish, but by its effects upon the body-politic as a whole. ' There are many things in reformation,' he said in 1780, when discussing parliamentary reform, ' which would be proper to be done, if other things can be done along with them ; but which, if they cannot be so accompanied, ought not to be done at all.' [1] The caution that underlies the words, it may be granted, became excessive. Nay, let it be said at once, it passed into the political valetudinarianism which shrinks from touching even the insignificant parts of a constitution from a nervous fear of the far-reaching effects upon an organic whole so delicately balanced and so permeable to influence. Yet, if this be true, it does but accentuate the point before us. When we laugh at the valetudinarian of private life, we need not grudge him the true perception, hidden sometimes from his robuster neighbours, that the human body is an organic whole. Similarly in politics, fear of reform is often enough far more than the blind panic of alarmists for what may happen to this particular institution or that, this particular interest or that, with which they may chance to have thrown in their lot. It may come also, in worthier and more patriotic form, from the entirely true perception that, in matters social, to act upon the part

[1] Letter on the Duration of Parliaments.

is inevitably to influence the whole, and that no serious reforms are circumscribed in their effects within the horizon and control of their authors. This is what Burke saw from the outset of his career. Again and again, with a reiteration which, but for the varied splendours of his rhetoric, would be wearisome, he claims that he always looked at his country and its institutions as a whole. 'The diversified but connected fabric of universal justice'—so runs his declaration to the electors of Bristol in 1780—'is well cramped and bolted together in all its parts ; and depend upon it I have never employed, and I never shall employ, any engine of power which may come into my hands to wrench it asunder. All shall stand, if I can help it, and all shall stand connected.' This runs throughout ; and its result is natural enough. It led him to magnify, perhaps beyond all other political writers, the dangers as well as the difficulties of reform ; and eventually, we must add, to think, not without contempt and fury, that the radical theorists, in the darkness of their fancied illumination, were grotesquely ignorant of the magnitude and perils of the task to which they had set their hands. To put it plainly, they did not know what they were doing ; because, in their concern for man's rights, they forgot his nature, and in their raw haste to reform understood neither the complexity nor the vulnerability of the society they were reforming. This did not prevent him from

saying with entire sincerity to the end of his days
that there was a time for reform. He never went
back upon that. But it certainly brought him, in
his later years, to resist and denounce wellnigh
every reformer with whom he found himself confronted.

All this, however, may well seem so far from convincing as rather to provoke a question. For what,
we may ask, has become of the human mind which
Burke so frankly recognised as ' the proximate
efficient cause ' of events ? Has he not admitted its
initiative ? Has he not said, on many a warning
page, that it can even work havoc with civilisation ? If so, it is surely not rash to believe that it
can do something. And if it can do so much as even
reform a representative system, not to say carry
through a revolution, as in 1688 it did, why should
it be thought a thing impossible that radical minds
and radical ideals should build up the democratic
state ? If a common soldier or a girl at the
door of an inn can change the course of history,
is there no room for the combined energies of radical
reformers ?

To such questions as these it is not easy to find
a completely satisfying answer in Burke. He recognises the proximate efficient causation of the human
mind so explicitly in the life of states that he makes
it difficult to see why there should be so little room
for it in even thoroughgoing reconstructive work.

He can speak with eloquence, as we have seen,[1] of
what one vigorous mind, confiding in the aid of God
and his own fortitude, can do in averting calamity,
by rallying supporters to his side. Why, then, it is
natural to ask, should this be the monopoly of the
conservative spirit ? Nay, was not Burke himself
a reformer ? ' He was no enemy to reformation.
Almost every business in which he was much concerned, from the first day he sat in that House
to that hour, was a business of reformation ; and
when he had not been employed in correcting, he
had been employed in resisting abuses ' [2]—this is
what he said of himself in a speech in the House in
1790: And the best illustrative comment on his
words is a list drawn up by Buckle of the measures
of reform to which he put his hand.

' Not only did he attack the absurd laws against
forestalling and regrating, but by advocating the
freedom of trade, he struck at the root of all similar
prohibitions. He supported those just claims of the
Catholics which, during his lifetime, were obstin-
ately refused ; but which were conceded, many years
after his death, as the only means of preserving the
integrity of the empire. He supported the petition
of the Dissenters, that they might be relieved from
the restrictions to which, for the benefit of the
Church of England, they were subjected. Into other
departments of politics he carried the same spirit.

[1] P. 64.   [2] Speech on the Army Estimates, 1790.

He opposed the cruel laws against insolvents by which, in the time of George III., our statute-book was still defaced ; and he vainly attempted to soften the penal code, the increasing severity of which was one of the worst features of that bad reign. He wished to abolish the old plan of enlisting soldiers for life—a barbarous and impolitic practice, as the English legislature began to perceive several years later. He attacked the slave-trade, which, being an ancient usage, the king wished to preserve as part of the British constitution. He refuted, but owing to the prejudices of the age, was unable to subvert, the dangerous power exercised by the judges, who, in criminal prosecutions for libel, confined the jury to the mere question of publication, thus taking the real issue into their own hands, and making themselves the arbiters of the fate of those who were so unfortunate as to be placed at their bar. And, what many will think not the least of his merits, he was the first in that long line of financial reformers to whom we are deeply indebted. Notwithstanding the difficulties thrown in his way, he carried through Parliament a series of Bills by which several useless places were entirely abolished, and, in the single office of paymaster-general, a saving effected to the country of £25,000 a year.' [1]

This is a notable record, and in the light of it, as supplement to his general doctrine as to the

[1] Buckle's *History of Civilisation*, vol. i. p. 462.

causation of the human mind, it is the most natural thing in the world that the reader of Burke should feel inclined to press the question why the radical reformers who followed Price or Paine should be resisted and vilified, when they were only doing their best to carry reform into the political constitution with the same thoroughness with which Burke himself had dealt with matters—slavery, for instance, or freeing of trade, or economic reform— not less important to the happiness of a people.

This question, however, is not without its answer ; and this lies along quite definite lines. It turns, in fact, upon the two closely related convictions : *firstly*, that a civil society, just because it is a highly developed organism, is peculiarly vulnerable ; and *secondly*, that though the minds and wills of men may play their part, and that part far from slight, in the growth and conservation of states, they may be all too easily perverted into the instruments of social disintegration and misery. For not only was Burke, with the wide outlook of a student of history, alive to the fact that nations and even civilisations have perished in the past, and may perish in the future ; he came to believe, especially in the lurid light of events in France, that they may disintegrate with an incalculable and calamitous rapidity. It is easy to say that his fears were excessive ; easy to contend (in the light of what has happened since) that neither England nor Europe was really on the

brink of the ' red ruin and the breaking up of laws,'
which was his dream by night and his spectre by
day; easy to point out that the conjuncture of
conditions which precipitated events in France did
not exist in Great Britain. Yet it does not follow
that his fears were theoretically unreasonable. For
what is it but the truth, and not a little of the
tragedy of human life is due to it, that all the slow
and hardly won results of organic growth may be
in many ways undone at a stroke ? It is so in
vegetable and animal life, when blight and parasit-
ism do their swift, insidious work. It is so with a
human character which, fashioned by the fostering
care of years, may be precipitated towards declen-
sion by a single, sudden, grievous lapse. It is so in
commerce, when a great business, built up by years
of industry, may be ruined by the speculative folly
of an hour. Is it not so also in the life of states, in
which the sensitive complexity of social structure
offers to the turbulent wills of their members opportunities of working mischief on the largest scale ?
For it is not to be denied that human wills may assert
themselves in what Burke regarded as a fatally
wrong way. They may shut their eyes to the
experience of the past, and scoff at the teaching of
history, as Paine and Godwin and Bentham did.
They may glory, as these men gloried, in an ignorant
irreverence for ancient institutions. They may
prefer, with light hearts, to fling all their energies

into new beginnings ; and if they have the courage
of their convictions, they may proceed, after the
fashion of the men of 1789, to realise their ideals
forthwith, if need be, by pike and guillotine. It is
at such times that states may be undone by the very
agencies, the wills of men, which, duly restrained
and rightly directed, might have become the proximate causes of national strength, stability, and
happiness. This was the fear that seems to have
haunted Burke in his later years. His conception
of society as organic never led him to think that
constitutions grow like plants or animals, or to fail
to realise that political parties, and even individuals,
can leave their mark on a social system. But he
also realised, with an acute perception, that interference with a social system is one thing, and the
control of the results of interference another. Too
many, it is to be feared, fail to recognise the depth
of the distinction. For it is the snare of all reformers
to succumb to the illusion that their control of the
movements which they initiate is in proportion to
the energy, honesty, and hopefulness of their initiative. They fail to make allowance for the extent
to which the life of a nation all the while goes on its
own way, not of course uninfluenced by the efforts
of politicians to direct it, yet nevertheless obedient
to forces which remain imperfectly under control.
Statesmen have before now enacted a Corn Law—
to discover after many days that they were starving

a people ; or passed a Poor Law—to leave posterity
to find out that they were pauperising a community.
Or a company of merchants have established a
trading company, all unaware that they were
annexing a dependency or preparing the way for
a protectorate. Or reformers may press forward
radical measures till they have, all unwittingly,
pressed them across the line that parts reform from
revolution. One may not say that the initiative is
easy, but it is sometimes child's play as compared
with the control of what has been initiated. For
there is a chemistry of politics as well as of labora-
tories ; and the new combinations of human elements and reagents may liberate, if not create,
unexpected forces such as even the most far-sighted
political manipulators cannot foresee, and still less
control. Beyond a doubt Danton and Robe-
spierre believed they were reconstructing the French
state ; what neither they nor the collective wisdom
of the Convention saw was that they were unchaining
a spirit which was, in brief space, to carry them
whither they would not, and to end by devouring
them and their following. ' How unknown is a
man, or a body of men to itself,' exclaims Carlyle,
moralising upon the irony of Fate that used the
revolutionists for its purposes, not for theirs. It
was no abnormal phenomenon. It is a commonplace, because it is a common experience, of all
political life that political forces seldom observe

the limits or follow the forecasts of those who set them in motion.

It is at any rate in reflections such as these that we must seek the explanation of the distrust, and even the terror, of all root and branch work which at once illumined and darkened the later post-Revolution years of Burke's life. For never by the methods of the Jacobins, nor by any approximation thereto, was it possible, according to his life-long conception of human affairs, for any genuine amelioration of man's lot to be achieved. The facts of human nature, the constitution of a people, the laws of social growth were all against it. The thing might, of course, be tried, but it could not be done. For of nothing was Burke more convinced, in his energies of reform no less than in his energies of resistance to reform, than that no political work could stand, nor any people advance by a single step towards happiness, unless reform, if reform must needs come, was cautious, gradual, reverent of the past, appreciative of the present, and ruled by the central principle that the actual performance of the constitution, whatever its defects, was immeasurably preferable to the untried projects and promises of radical reformers.

We have still, however, to see that what for these reasons was judged impracticable was likewise deemed undesirable. The attempt must fail. But, for other reasons besides the certainty of failure,

with all the disasters it was sure to carry in its
train, the attempt ought never to be made. This
is a point of vital moment. For it brings us
back[1] to the fact that Burke's conservatism was
begotten not only of the analogies of organic growth,
nor of his generalised knowledge of men and affairs,
nor yet of his fears of radical ' architects of ruin,'
but of his religious convictions.

(b) *The Undesirability of Radical Reform*

For the last word, and the deepest, of Burke's
conservatism has not yet been said. If it were so,
his political doctrine would be written only in two
chapters ; the alarmist chapter of fears, and the
persuasive chapter which would convince us that,
by the very constitution of human nature on the
one hand, and of civil society on the other, advance
must inevitably be slow ; fear of the ruin rash wills
may work, and acceptance of those actualities of
social existence which come fortified by the analogy
of organisms, and accredited by the wisdom and
experience of past generations.

But Burke's horizon as a thinker is not thus
limited. He moves, as we have said, in a larger
and more philosophical orbit. Nor does he rest
till he has linked on his conception of a people
to those presuppositions of sweeping generality
already indicated—none other than those involved

[1] P. 14.

in the assumption that the course of history and the
destinies of nations are guided by the providence of
God, and that therefore the constitution of a state
is ultimately the result of spiritual forces which are
eternal and supreme. Writers on Burke have
rightly dwelt on his preference for the historical
method, on his constant appeal to the experience of
men and nations, on his fruitful application of biological analogies to the state. And, justifiably
enough, they have on these grounds enrolled him in
the ranks of inductive historical thinkers.[1] But the
truth is (as we have already ventured to suggest)
that, in the last resort, his method is deductive.
What else can be said of a thinker who not only
avows a passionate theistic creed, but applies this
creed with such assiduity that neither his conservative faith nor his conservative fear can be adequately understood apart from it ? Nothing can
be more evident, indeed, than that Burke's political teaching, however firmly grounded in historical
and analogical methods, does not find its final
explanation in them.

This, to be sure, is a strong statement. But
will any reader of Burke condemn it as too strong,
when he recalls the sustained and closely reasoned
passage—and it is only one of many lesser passages

[1] *E.g.* Professor Graham, who in his *English Political Philosophy* calls the *Reflections* 'the first English book in which the
new Historical Method of inquiry and explanation is employed,'
p. 92.

—in which this linking-up of political doctrine to religious faith finds its fullest expression. It comes in the context of the *Appeal from the New to the Old Whigs*, when he is urging the characteristic and highly conservative doctrine that it is the situation of the individual, far more truly than his choice, that is the arbiter of his duties :

' Taking it for granted that I do not write to the disciples of the Parisian philosophy, I may assume that the awful Author of our being is the Author of our place in the order of existence ; and that, having disposed and marshalled us by a Divine tactic, not according to our will, but according to His, He has in and by that disposition, virtually subjected us to act the part which belongs to the place assigned us. We have obligations to mankind at large, which are not in consequence of any special voluntary pact. They arise from the relation of man to man, and the relation of man to God, which relations are not matters of choice. On the contrary, the force of all the pacts which we enter into with any particular person or number of persons amongst mankind depends upon those prior obligations. In some cases the subordinate relations are voluntary, in others they are necessary —but the duties are all compulsive. When we marry, the choice is voluntary, but the duties are not matter of choice. They are dictated by the nature of the situation. Dark and inscrutable are the ways by which we come into the world. The instincts which give rise to this mysterious process of nature are not of our making. But out of physical causes, unknown to us, perhaps unknowable, arise moral duties which, as we are able perfectly to comprehend, we are bound indispensably to perform. Parents may not be consenting to their moral relation ; but, consenting or not, they are bound to a long train of burthensome duties towards those with whom they have never made a convention of any sort. Children are not consenting to their relation, but their relation, without their actual consent, binds them to its duties ; or rather it implies their consent, because the presumed consent of every rational creature is in unison with the predisposed order of things.' And the whole passage (which cannot further be quoted) winds up with the words : ' If you ask, *Quem te Deus esse jussit ?* you will be answered when you resolve this other question, *Humana qua parte locatus es in re ?* ' [1]

It is impossible to regard this as other than one of the most important passages in Burke's writings. The more so because it is only what we might expect from the study of his life. For religion was from first to last so central a fact in his outlook upon the world that it would be strange indeed if he were minded to leave it on the shore when he embarked on the sea of politics. It is needless to enlarge on this. His own avowals are decisive : ' We know, and what

[1] *Appeal.*

is better, we feel inwardly that religion is the basis of civil society, and the source of all good and of all comfort.'[1] ' On that religion,' he declares elsewhere, referring to Christianity, ' according to our mode, all our laws and institutions stand as upon their base.'[2]

Hence we may expect to find, and indeed it would be wonderful were it otherwise, that this theistic faith not only colours but saturates his political doctrine through and through. Far more, indeed, than a reader might gather from the many wise and charming pages by which Lord Morley has earned the gratitude of every student of Burke—if one may venture thus to suggest what savours of criticism of a conscript father of literature. ' This brings me,' says Lord Morley, ' to remark a really singular trait. In spite of the predominance of practical sagacity, of the habits and spirit of public business, of vigorous actuality in Burke's character, yet at the bottom of all his thoughts about communities and governments there lay a certain mysticism. . . . He was using no otiose epithet, when he described the disposition of a stupendous wisdom " moulding together the great mysterious incorporation of the human race." To him there actually was an element of mystery in the cohesion of men in societies, in political obedience, in the sanctity of contract ; in all that fabric of law and charter and obligation, whether

[1] *Reflections.*   [2] *Regicide Peace*, Letter IV.

written or unwritten, which is the sheltering bul-
wark between civilisation and barbarism. When
reason and history had contributed all that they
could to the explanation, it seemed to him as if the
vital force, the secret of organisation, the binding
framework, must still come from the impenetrable
regions beyond reasoning and beyond history.' [1]

In one particular this passage is unimpeachable.
It recognises explicitly enough the theistic meta-
physic that lies behind Burke's politics. But why
should this be regarded as ' a really singular trait ? '
Practicality and religious faith are not necessarily
divorced. Grant that to many minds theism and
politics lie far apart, and that from some minds the
theism has vanished. Yet these two classes do not
exhaust the universe of political discourse. Certainly the philosophers of history, both in France
and Germany, have for the most part regarded it as
neither singular nor impossible to find a place for
Divine agency in human affairs. And, apart from
them, what are we to say of Plato, Coleridge, Hegel,
Carlyle, Mazzini, and T. H. Green ? They are diverse
enough, and their diversity makes it all the more
striking that they are at one in being constrained,
by such light of reason as was in them, to discern in
the political life of nations the action of more than
merely secular forces. None of these, hardly even
Carlyle, was much in love with ' the impenetrable

[1] *Burke* in ' English Men of Letters,' p. 165.

regions beyond reasoning,' if there be such. None
of them ever doubted that Reason assured him that
society rests on spiritual foundations. To ignore
this would be to dismiss spiritual idealism without
a hearing.

Similarly with Burke. The vision of God, the
faith in ' stupendous wisdom,' the belief in a ' Divine
tactic ' in history were inwoven with his whole interpretation of experience and outlook on the world.
And though, being neither theologian nor meta-
physician, he never dreamed of proving these convictions (therein, no doubt, disclosing his limits as
a thinker), this does not touch the fact that he carried
them with him, with a passionate insistence, into
his politics. Apart from them his thought and his
utterance are in large measure unintelligible.

This becomes evident when we recall the intensity
of his antipathy to radical reform. For his contention here is not merely that reformers can do
little to construct, however easy they may find it
to destroy, but that, beyond comparatively narrow
limits, they ought not to try. The limitations he
would lay upon them are more than those imposed
by the practical difficulties and dangers of their
attempts. They are moral and religious. They
arise from the fact that ' the place of every man
determines his duty,' and that these duties of one's
station are to be accepted, not because we cannot,
if we will, revolt against them, but because in respect

of the fundamental relationships at any rate, we have been ' disposed and marshalled by a Divine tactic,' and thereby ' virtually subjected to act the part which belongs to the place assigned us.' Few writers have gone further than Burke in this direction. Almost, at times, he would persuade us that it is a sin to lay a finger on the ark of the constitution. He tells us that ' duties are not voluntary ' : he adds that ' duty and will are even contradictory terms ' ; [1] and though we may quarrel with the ethical terminology, it is none the less well fitted to emphasise the rigour of the restraints of moral and political, which are also for him those of religious, obligation. Nor is this a merely general attitude. On the contrary it determines his position in respect of specific questions of the first magnitude. We may take these, briefly, in turn, and first that reverence for the past which is perhaps the characteristic of Burke's writings best known to the general reader.

[1] *Appeal.*

CHAPTER VI

THE WISDOM OF OUR ANCESTORS

In nothing is Burke more pre-eminently in harmony with the spirit of the nineteenth century than in that reverence for the past, for lack of which the writers of the eighteenth have been severely handled even by latter-day radicals. 'No one,' says Mill, in his great essay on Coleridge, 'can calculate what struggles, which the cause of improvement has yet to undergo, might have been spared, if the philosophers of the eighteenth century had done anything like justice to the past.' Burke at any rate did justice to it. His very name is a symbol for reverence towards all that is old and venerable. Who has not met the familiar words that 'people will not look forward to posterity who never look backward to their ancestors'? Who fails to recognise the almost equally familiar declaration: 'We fear God; we look up with awe to kings; with affection to parliaments; with duty to magistrates; with reverence to priests; and with respect to nobility'? And what reader can forget the passages which come crowding on the memory in defence and laudation of

prescription ?   ' Prescription is the most solid of all
titles, not only to property, but, which is to secure
that property, to government.'   ' All titles ter-
minate in prescription.'   ' Nor is prescription of
government formed upon blind unmeaning prejudices—for man is a most unwise and most wise
being.   The individual is foolish ; . . . but the species
is wise, and when time is given to it, as a species it
almost always acts right.' [1]   Nor does he hesitate
again and again to hold a brief even for prejudice,
which indeed, if only it be inveterate, has never had
an apologist to equal him.   ' Prejudice,' he writes,
' is of ready application in the emergency ; it pre-
viously engages the mind in a steady course of wisdom and virtue, and does not leave the man hesitat-
ing in the moment of decision, sceptical, puzzled,
and unresolved.   Prejudice renders a man's virtue
his habit ; and not a series of unconnected acts.
Through just prejudice, his duty becomes a part of
his nature.' [2] He even goes a step further.   Nothing
is easier than to find sentences in which he urges
what sounds like a surrender of individual judgment
altogether in the presence of principles and institutions which come clothed in the loyalties and
experiences of successive generations.   Three may
suffice.   In one he declares himself obliged ' by an
infinitely overwhelming balance of authority, to
prefer the collective wisdom of ages to the abilities

[1] Speech, May 7, 1782.   [2] *Reflections.*

of any two men living.' [1]   In the second he makes
the characteristic confession : ' We are afraid to put
men to live and trade each on his own private stock
of reason ; . . . individuals would do better to
avail themselves of the general bank and capital
of nations and of ages.' [2]   The third is even more
pronounced : ' Thanks to our sullen resistance to
innovation, thanks to the cold sluggishness of our
national character, we still bear the stamp of our
forefathers. . . . We know that *we* have made no
discoveries, and we think that no discoveries are to
be made, in morality ; nor many in the great principles of government, nor in the ideas of liberty, which
were understood long before we were born, altogether as well as they will be after the grave has
heaped its mould upon our presumption, and the
silent tomb shall have imposed its law on our pert
loquacity.' [3]

It is needless, however, to labour this point.
These passages are sufficient to justify us in taking
many others to a like effect as read, and in going
on to inquire into the grounds upon which this
reverential, and, as some might think, this all too
deferential attitude to the past may be said to
rest. And this is the more important because it
is so easy to surrender to the notion (not, one sus-
pects, uncommon) that Burke is simply the prejudiced prophet of authority—the authority of usages

[1] *Regicide Peace*, Letter III.   [2] *Reflections.*   [3] *Ibid.*

and institutions and beliefs that stand sponsored by
old use and wont and the wisdom of ancestors.

This, however, would be a flagrant misinter-
pretation. For, if we are to characterise Burke by
a single epithet, that epithet would not be apostle
of authority. As already suggested,[1] it would be
apostle of 'prudence.' Grant that the appeal to
prescription is strong, sweeping, and at times almost
unqualified; it is nevertheless not final. It does
not really involve the deposition of that reason
which he declared, as we have seen,[2] to be alone
'sovereign' in all matters political. For, when all
is said, it is not reverence that is the mother of the
virtues ; it is 'prudence.' And where this virtue
of the practical reason is supreme, there can be no
such thing as the *surrender* of the judgment in
presence even of the most venerated authorities.
That this holds true of Burke we can see in more
ways than one. We can see it, for example, in
his handling of precedents. Of course he is fond of
citing precedents. One of the greatest of his pieces,
the *Appeal from the New to the Old Whigs*, suggests
this by its very title. And it lies on the surface
that he assigns to precedents a value which was to
Tom Paine a stumbling-block, and to Bentham
foolishness. But he is not for that reason to be
confused with those lawyers of politics to whom a
precedent is a solution. 'Cases,' he says, 'are dead

[1] P. 38 *et seq.*   [2] P. 42.

things, principles are living and productive.' [1]   For
the genuine value of precedents, on his view of them,
lies not in their being reproducible in the letter,
which indeed is usually impossible in face of changed
circumstances, but in their serving to enlighten the
practical judgment, as object-lessons of the ways
in which men of affairs go to meet their problems.
Nor does it need much proof that the man whose
practical judgment is alive, the man in whom
' prudence ' is truly the mother of the political
virtues, is at the opposite pole from that of the
precedent-ridden lawyer of politics. ' Legislators
ought to do what lawyers cannot.' [2]

The same line of thought recurs in Burke's estimate of the value of the study of history. He loved
history. He even aspired to write history. But
this did not prevent him from laughing at the
shallow partisans who would degrade history into
an arsenal of controversial weapons, or from despis-
ing the pedants who, blind to the incalculable
combinations of circumstance, expect to find in the
past ready-made solutions of difficulties which
every man of affairs must meet for himself. ' Not
that I derogate from the use of history. It is a
great improver of the understanding, by showing
both men and affairs in a great variety of views.
From this source much political wisdom may be
learned ; that is, may be learned as habit, not as

---

[1] *Observations.*   [2] Letter to the Sheriffs.

precept ; and as an exercise to strengthen the mind
as furnishing materials to enlarge and enrich it, not
as a repertory of cases and precedents for a lawyer :
if it were, a thousand times better would it be that
a statesman had never learned to read.' [1]

Similarly in his attitude towards the authority of
great names or venerable institutions: though reverential to the verge of superstition, it is not slavish.
He never abdicates, nor would he have any statesman abdicate, his rational judgment. ' Prudence
in new cases,' he says, ' can do nothing on grounds
of retrospect.' [2]   And if, as in some of the passages
cited above, he counsels a self-distrust which is not
easy to distinguish from surrender, this attitude
was one which he was firmly convinced was dictated by reason itself.   For his liturgy to the past
is inspired not by the mere love of bygone things—
he protests again and again that he is no antiquarian
—nor yet, in more than part, by the sentiment and
romance that gathered round all that was old and
venerable to a mind like Scott's.   It has a deeper,
a more practical, and a more rational root in two
further convictions which go hand-in-hand in his
scheme of things.

(a) The one of these is that every institution,
nay, every prejudice that has long held its ground,
is a deposit of experience—the experience which

---

[1] *Remarks on the Policy of the Allies.*
[2] *Thoughts on French Affairs.*

the many minds and hands of successive generations have been hoarding up in ' the bank and capital
of nations, and of the ages.' Here are his words :
' Then what is the standard of expedience ?   Expedience is that which is good for the community
and good for every individual in it.   Now, this
expedience is the desideratum to be sought either
without the experience of means, or with that
experience.   If without, as in the case of the fabri-
cation of a new commonwealth, I will hear the
learned arguing what promises to be expedient; but
if we are to judge of a commonwealth actually
existing, the first thing I enquire is what has been
found expedient or inexpedient.   And I will not
take their *promise* rather than the *performance* of
the constitution.' [1]   Nowhere is his position put
with greater clearness.   Expedience is the ultimate
end.   So far his face was to the future.   So far he
was, in a sense,[2] a utilitarian.   But to this there
are two qualifications : the one—on which enough
has been said—that expedience always means, in
his vocabulary, what is expedient for a people as
an organic whole ; the other, that it is only in and
through the long and gradual process of social
organisation that discovery is made of the institutions and the principles of civil and religious liberty
whereby the expedient can best be realised.   Not
that he ever thought ' the performance of the

[1] Speech, May 7, 1782.   [2] P. 49.

constitution' to be faultless. He was well aware
that perfection was not to be found in it, nor in any
other human contrivance. No, he was only convinced that with all its corruptions, to which he
by no means closed his eyes, it had experimentally
proved itself immeasurably better than anything
that radical reform had to put in its place.

(b) But, then, we must not suppose that experience, ' the arguments of states and kingdoms ' as
he called it, weighed for so much simply because it
embodied the experience of ancestors. There was
the further reason that the experience of a people,
as disclosed in the course of its history, was regarded
by him as providentially guided. In his eyes it
was nothing less than ' the known march of the
ordinary providence of God.' [1]   Had it been merely
secular experience, it would have been much ; but
as experience with the Divine imprimatur, it was
immeasurably more.

It is here that Burke is at the opposite pole to
that of the radicals, both of his own day and of that
which was immediately to follow. The past was
nothing to them. To the irreverent soul of Paine
history was nothing but a horrid spectacle of
' ruffian torturing ruffian.' To the practical mind
of Bentham, to whom the ' wisdom of ancestors '
was the wisdom of the cradle, it was of value only

---

[1] 'The rules of prudence, which are formed upon the known
march of the ordinary providence of God.'—*Regicide Peace*,
Letter II.

in so far as something might be learnt from its
follies and its crimes. Nor was it enough for Burke
to escape these lamentable limitations by insisting,
as Mill did at a later day, that reformers must learn
to do justice to the past, or, with the evolutionists
of the nineteenth century, that past and present are
inseparable phases of one continuous development.
Nothing could satisfy him short of the faith that
the whole drama of a nation's life was the revelation
of a 'Divine tactic.' He does not prove his point.
He does not dream of attempting to prove it. He
made no claim to furnish a philosophy of history.
But there can be no doubt at all that it was an
unalterable conviction, apart from which his profound reverence for the past can neither be understood nor justified.

Hence, too, the peculiar passion of detestation
which all too freely suffused his polemic against
the radical reformers for their contempt for the
lessons of history. Not only were they setting at
nought the experience of their species ; they were
guilty, in his eyes, of a kind of practical atheism.
Hence, too, the ferocity of his invective. It is not
politics. It is not toleration. It is not charity.
But it is intelligible. For he who habitually sees
in the constitution under which he rejoices to live
nothing less than the handiwork of God, will certainly be more tempted than his more secularly
minded neighbours to denounce radical reforms as

'prodigies of sacrilege.' This, of course, must not be taken to mean that he stigmatised all radicals as atheists, though the word flows so easily from his pen as almost to suggest it. On the contrary he remarks, when assailing Dr. Price in the *Reflections*, that the signal for revolutions has often been given from pulpits. But there can be no doubt at all that he regarded radicalism, whether in pulpits or out of them, as both in its principles and methods antagonistic to 'the known march of the ordinary providence of God.'

It is this indeed which raises one of the most serious difficulties which the student of Burke encounters. So masterful is the force of his religious faith, that it becomes difficult to reconcile his fears for the future with a faith so masterful. For if the experience of the past bears witness so convincingly to Divine plan and agency, this surely might seem to carry the suggestion that the political theories of radicalism, especially if they be as ill-grounded as he declares them to be, are not likely to seriously turn aside the march of the providence of God. Is the arm of omnipotence to be shortened? Is Divine control to cease with the eighteenth century of the Christian era? Is Whig ascendency the one way given under heaven and among men for political salvation? If the essence of religion be, as it has been well defined, a 'faith in the conservation of values,' why all these dire forebodings that all that

is most precious in England, and even in civilisation,
will crumble and perish before radical assault ?
These are questions that cannot be repressed. Nor
are they questions which it is easy to answer. For
if Divine agency in human affairs is to be invoked
at all, it must be supposed to operate continuously
and throughout. And if it be affirmed, as by Burke
it is affirmed, that it has operated all through the
past, so that its achieved results are the object of
all but idolatry, it might not unreasonably be
inferred that it would need something more deadly
than radicals and radical ideals, which after all
Burke himself not seldom treats with contempt,
to plunge the future in a godless anarchy.

Burke's inferences, however, took a different
direction. At an early stage he had come to the
conviction, which steadily grew upon him to the
end of his days, that the Revolution was something
far more formidable than a merely political movement. In its inspiration, in its leaders, in its aims,
he believed it to have struck an unholy alliance
with infidelity and atheism. He calls it 'atheism by
establishment.' [1] Nor did he entertain the shadow of
a doubt that, were it suffered to run its course, it
would not only subvert political institutions but rob
the world of its religious faith. And whatever he may
have thought of the avowed theism of Rousseau or
Price or Paine, of which he cannot have been ignor-

[1] *Regicide Peace*, Letter i.

ant, it certainly did nothing, even in the slightest degree, to qualify this forecast. The result followed. His religious faith in the providence of God in history, which we might expect would have allayed his fears, had an opposite effect. It intensified them. As the manifest object of revolutionary assault, it gave a deeper and more menacing significance to the radical attack upon political institutions. For it is never to be forgotten that a religious faith was, for Burke, far more than ' the source of all hope and all comfort ' to private lives ; it was also, and always, the foundation ' upon which all our laws and institutions stand as upon their base.' This must be already evident ; but it will be more evident still when we turn to his uncompromising insistence upon the limits of Discussion and Toleration.

CHAPTER VII

THE LIMITATIONS OF DISCUSSION AND TOLERATION

(a) *The Limits of Political Discussion*

THERE is much in Burke's life to encourage the expectation that he would prove himself an apostle of free discussion. Few men of his day, not even Johnson, indulged in discussion more than he. We know from Boswell how discussion ranged and raged at the club : the sound of it re-echoes still. And none of us can forget that tribute, wrung from the dictator who nightly bore all down before him, though to be sure it was only because he felt himself below par when he made the admission : ' That fellow calls forth all my powers. Were I to see Burke now, it would kill me.' Nor were these evenings of the gods limited to topics political. For though the keen wits and good-fellowship that gathered together at the Turk's Head were in a measure restrained from the audacities, irresponsibilities and levities which, among the *illuminati* of French salons, as well as in the obscurer circles of the English free-thinkers, of whom Godwin and his friends were typical, pushed argument and epigram freely into the spiritual world, even a cursory glance at Boswell's pages is proof that the range was wide. And, when we turn to politics, we have already seen how, all his life through, Burke could not deal with any question without pushing it far into the region of principles. No man, it is safe to say, ever discussed politics as he did, none so persistently, none with such eloquence and penetration, none with more determination to go to the root of the matter. In his later years, when the Revolution had still more freely opened up the ways of utterance, he could hardly discuss anything else than the very foundations of civil society. Whatever the topic, it was always, in these later days of fiery controversy, sure to return to that.

And yet it is not to Burke that we must go to find the case for freedom of discussion. He is not to be classed, in this respect, with Milton or Mill. Not freedom to discuss, but the limits which discussion is bound to recognise—this is the central theme.

This was doubtless due, in part at any rate, to what he saw on a visit to France. For he had gone over to Paris in 1773, and had seen there at close quarters the spectacle of a society in which everything was discussed—a society which, to use Lord Morley's words, ' babbled about God and state of nature, about virtue and the spirituality of the soul, much as Boswell may have done when Johnson complained of him for asking questions that would make a man hang himself.' [1] The impression left on the reverent spirit of Burke was indelibly repulsive. And, in due season, though not without a reinforcing revulsion against similar tendencies in England, it bore its fruit in the decisive declaration : ' It has been the misfortune (not, as these gentlemen think it, the glory) of this age that everything is to be discussed.' [2]

Why did he think so ? Why did this protagonist in discussion thus lift up his testimony against discussion ?

Partly, one can see, it is simply that familiar phenomenon, the practical man's impatience of endless debate, born of the perception that the zealot for criticism and discussion, in his fanatical inability to know when to desist, may, by the assertion of freedom to discuss, fatally obstruct that freedom to act which is of the essence of all liberty that is not to be volubly barren of deeds. Burke has put the point in a passage which might with advantage be engraved on the lintels of all latter-day legislative assemblies. Is it because it is so well known and taken for granted, that it has been so seldom quoted ? ' I must first beg leave just to hint to you that we may suffer very great detriment by being open to every talker. It is not to be imagined how much of service is lost from spirits full of

---

[1] Morley's *Rousseau*, p. 130.   [2] *Reflections.*

activity, and full of energy, who are pressing, who are rushing forward to great and capital issues, when you oblige them to be continually looking back. Whilst they are defending one service, they defraud you of a hundred. Applaud us when we run ; console us when we fall ; cheer us when we recover ; but let us pass on—for God's sake let us pass on.' [1] Seldom has the case against verbose obstruction and obstructive verbosity been so forcibly put.

This, however, is rather a question of common sense and tactics than of principle. It is a different and a more serious matter when we turn to the kind of discussion that takes the form of political casuistry ; for of political casuistry Burke has not only a rooted but a reasoning suspicion. Not that he could, or would, rule it altogether out. Like every student of history and every man of affairs, he is well aware that cases occur—difficult cases, critical cases, casuistical cases, in which it seems impossible to do the right without doing violence to some time-honoured obligation. It is so, clearly enough, in the hour of impending revolution, when men are asking themselves fearfully if the Rubicon has to be crossed ; and, far short of this, it is so also when the honest citizen finds himself in conscientious conflict with the behests of his party, the policy of his country, and the law of the land. None knew

[1] Speech at Bristol, 1780.

better than Burke that such emergencies must be faced and dealt with. He was not blind to the fact that even revolutions must sometimes come. How could he be, when from first to last he was the apologist of 1688 ? How could he be, when he discussed the whole question of the revolt of the American colonies as it never has been discussed ? And when the catastrophe of 1789 burst upon Europe, least of all men did he fail to face it, and discuss it to the uttermost. The thing he feared and hated was, therefore, not that even supreme issues should be discussed, when events had forced them to the front, but that they should be rashly raised and cried upon the house-tops by irresponsible politicians (or those he took to be such), who, without the justification of dire emergency, were ready to raise questions that went to the roots of political allegiance. This was the accusation he fastened on the radicals. They were all alike in his eyes, traffickers in extremes and rash dabblers in a pernicious political casuistry. They were for ever calling in question the fundamental obligations of civil society ; for ever preaching up the rights of revolution ; for ever arguing in ultimatums ; for ever eager to administer the extreme medicine of the state as if it were its daily bread. This was what Burke denounced with an unsparing invective. He had a horror of it that is all but morbid ; for, in his eyes, it could eventuate in only one result. It would destroy for ever that unsuspecting confidence in the law and the constitution, upon which all political stability reposed. It would leave nothing that was not to be called in question. It would habituate men's minds to the thought of the violation of obligations which ought never to be shaken, except when the worst comes to the worst. It would end, to use his own pregnant words, by ' turning men's duties into doubts.' At a later day, Mill was to plead for all but unlimited discussion as the great vitaliser of convictions, and as the one adequate security against ' the profound slumber of a decided opinion.' But Burke could see little of this. The ' profound slumber of a decided opinion ' was so far from carrying any terrors for him that it was rather welcomed as a symptom of political health. That ideas should become convictions, and convictions sentiments, nay, even that sentiments should pass into prejudices (if the prejudices were just)—this was the condition of moral and social stability. And, by consequence, to shake this wholesome settledness of mind by the doubts and discussions of political casuistry, was the sure path to the undoing of the State. ' I confess to you, sir, I never liked this continual talk of resistance and revolution, or the practice of making the extreme medicine of the constitution its daily bread. It renders the habit of society dangerously valetudinarian ; it is taking periodical

doses of mercury sublimate, and swallowing down
repeated provocatives of cantharides to our love
of liberty.' [1]

Yet this is not the whole of Burke's case for
the limitation of discussion, for the passion of
his protests is not to be explained merely by the
fact that his conservative instincts and convictions
recoiled from calling in question fundamental
institutions. It turns on the further point that
these institutions, and the loyalties they evoked,
were always regarded by him as the work of that
'stupendous wisdom' by which the Disposer of all
things has been marshalling the human race not
according to their will, but according to His. For
from this it followed that, as soon as criticism and
controversy touched the fundamentals of the constitution, they became by implication an attack
on that faith in the Divine government of the world,
which, as we have seen, was the foundation of Burke's
political religion. For it is characteristic of the
religious mind to resent and resist assaults upon
its settled valuations even more than upon its
dogmas. And when, as in Burke's case, these
valuations are political, two results are apt to
follow—the radical onslaught upon venerated institutions comes to be viewed as if it were an attack
upon religion itself ; and sceptical assault upon
religious faith to be reprobated as undermining the

[1] *Reflections.*

basis of the constitution. Both results appear in Burke. He resents and resists radicalism when it would push discussion into constitutional principles which (he thinks) ought never to be called in question, because they stand sponsored not only by experience, but by Divine wisdom ; and he measures out short shrift to atheists and infidels, because, by striking at religious faith, they shake the foundations of civil society. The first of these results appears in his case for the limitations of political discussion ; the second will appear when we turn to the well-worn topic of toleration. The limitations upon it are not less firm. Few great thinkers, indeed, have gone so far in using incomparable powers of discussion in proving that toleration, as well as discussion, ought to have its limits.

(b) *The Limits of Toleration*

There is no writer in whom, were we free to select some passages and to reject others, toleration finds a nobler voice than in Burke. ' In proportion as mankind has become enlightened, the idea of religious persecution, under any circumstances, has been almost universally exploded by all good and thinking men.' [1] So he wrote in his tolerant *Tracts on the Popery Laws*. Nor would half-measures content him. Keenly alive to the distinction between the persecution of an ancient faith and the

[1] *Tracts on the Popery Laws*, c. iii.

more excusable suppression of new opinions such as
might possibly initiate bitter civil dissensions, he
is not in the least disposed to palliate what he
calls the ' rotten and hollow ' policy of a ' preventive
persecution ' of the latter.   The same spirit breathes
in other passages : ' I take toleration to be a part
of religion. I do not know which I would sacrifice.
I would keep them both.' [1] And in the spirit of
that utterance, he was ready to see some truth in
all forms of religious creed, and to recognise even
superstition as ' the religion of feeble minds.'
' Toleration,' he elsewhere declares, in words that
might seem conclusive, ' is good for all or it is good
for none.' [2]

And yet the same hand which wrote these catholic
avowals penned also two other sentences which have
a different ring. ' Against these ' (i.e. infidels) ' I
would have the laws rise in all their terrors. . . . I
would cut up the very root of atheism.' This is
one : the other is not less emphatic : ' The infidels
are outlaws of the constitution ; not of this country,
but of the human race. They are never, never to
be supported, never to be tolerated.' [3]

Those are ferocious sentences. But they are
not to be read on that account as if they were an
outburst of personal intolerance of atheistic or
infidel opinions as matter of private conviction.

[1] Speech on relief of Protestant Dissenters, 1773.
[2] Ibid.   [3] Ibid.

True though it be that Burke detested atheism and
infidelity, he was nevertheless in private life conspicuously tolerant in matters of religion. He
hated bigotry. He hated persecution. He prided
himself upon so doing. ' If ever there was anything
to which, from reason, nature, habit, and principle,
I am totally averse, it is persecution for conscientious difference in opinion.' Such is his avowal.
And in the light of it, and the story of his life, we
need not entertain a doubt that had he believed
atheism and infidelity to have no further significance than as matters of private opinion, he would
never have called upon the laws to rise in their
terrors, and cut them up by the root. It is a long
stride from hating opinions, with even a perfect
hatred, and invoking the law courts to extirpate
them.

But this is precisely what Burke never could
believe. Theism and Christianity were, in his
eyes, things more momentous far than the concerns
of private consciences. Not only was man, in his
psychology, ' by his constitution a religious animal,'
and not only was atheism ' against not only our
reason but our instincts,' religious belief was (as
we have seen) a central fact in his conception of the
life of the State ; ' the basis of civil society, and the
source of all good and all comfort.' [1] ' On that
religion,' we have already heard him say, referring

[1] *Reflections.*

to Christianity, ' according to our mode, all our laws and institutions stand as upon their base.' [1] These are his premises, and in due course comes the conclusion, drawn with an unfaltering confidence : ' Religion is so far, in my opinion, from being out of the province or duty of a Christian magistrate that it is, and ought to be, not only his care, but the principal thing in his care ; because it is one of the great bonds of human society.' [2]   And should it happen that this magisterial care should take the form of visiting the terrors of the law upon the atheist and the infidel, the justification must be sought on the public ground that this is the needful check upon a peculiarly insidious and deadly form of political incendiarism.

Burke's position here, it may be granted, has, now for some time, happily become untenable. Of all methods for strengthening the religious bond of human society the prosecution of free-thinkers is the most forlorn. Conviction in a court of law, whatever be the pains and penalties it carries in its train, is impotent to turn the atheist into a believer ; and the religious faith which claims as its peculiar glory that it rests on the spontaneous and unconstrained devotion of the soul to God, is not likely to be recognised as the source of all good and all comfort by seeking the ill-starred alliance of fines and imprisonment. Nor is the Christian

[1] *Regicide Peace*, Letter iv.   [2] Speech, May 11, 1792.

magistrate to be envied who betakes himself to that 'refutation by criminal justice,' which Burke declared to be the refutation that the writings of Tom Paine best deserved. He would quickly, in our modern world at any rate, find himself hewing a Hydra. The crafty and dishonest would easily evade him. The sincere and outspoken unbeliever would gain the dignity of the martyr for conscience' sake. The sceptics would rise in protest in the name of honest doubt. The constructive thinkers, strong in their faith in reason, and conscious it may be of the magnitude of their own departures from orthodoxy, would catch alarm at the substitution of force for argument. And, not least, society, in whose best interests this persecution by prosecution is, in Burke's view, justifiable, would be continually plunged into all the disintegrating embitterments of those conflicts between law and private judgment, law and conscience, law and individual reason, law and liberty, which furnish some of the most miserably memorable, as well as glorious chapters in human history. In truth, the case for a toleration wide enough to include even the aggressive atheist and the obtrusive infidel has, under the hands of the apostles of freedom of thought and discussion, become so strong, and almost so much a matter of course, that the wonder grows that a mind so rational as Burke's, and an experience so wide, should have advanced, and reiterated,

so monstrous a doctrine as that it is the duty of
the civil magistrate to cut up the root of atheism
and to brand infidels as outlaws of the constitution.
If only he had held fast, and enlarged, his own great
declaration, that toleration is ' good for all or good
for none ' !

There is, however, an explanation, and it appears
to lie in two considerations.

1. The first is that, notwithstanding all his
rationality, Burke never adequately recognised the
place and value of speculative truth, and the conditions of its pursuit, in national life.   Though his
own reason, in alliance with imagination, was, in
the political sphere, essentially constructive, this
seemingly never suggested to him that free-thought
in its larger range was constructive in its essence
and results. We have already seen that his estimate of ' modern philosophers ' was far from flattering ; and the same spirit appears in his belittlement
of the English deists. ' Who,' he contemptuously
asks, ' born within the last forty years, has read
one word of Collins and Toland and Tindall and
Chubb and Morgan, and that whole race who call
themselves Free-thinkers ? ' [1]   All his experience
apparently suggested that speculative reason makes
for the disintegration of belief. It raised questions ;
it shook the unsuspecting confidence of time-
honoured convictions ; it turned men's duties into

[1] *Reflections.*

doubts ; it bred 'refining speculatists' and dangerous atheists ; it led to Serbonian bogs. This was
what he had seen in Paris ; and this was what he
dreaded for England. And, against it all, he had
no faith in speculative philosophy to set as counter-
weight and corrective. He had early, and by
proclivity magnificently justified of its results,
turned away decisively from the speculative to the
practical life, and again and again he makes haste
to disclaim all pretensions to be a ' philosopher ' or
' professor of metaphysics.' And not without
reason. For, so far at any rate as appears in life
or writings, he had but little acquaintance with
the great constructive efforts of Greek philosophy,
and still less with the philosophical systems of the
Continent, which indeed were still far below the
horizon of the English mind. Neither with the
Scottish philosophers (despite the passing project
of refuting Hume) nor with the English moralists
did he much concern himself ; and if, on occasion,
we might trace the influence of Locke, it is the
Locke as the apologist of 1688, and not the Locke
of the *Essay on the Understanding*. In short he had
nothing wherewith to meet the solvents of the
' French philosophy ' he dreaded, except his own
reflections upon life, fortified by a wide outlook on
history, a large knowledge of literature, and a comprehensive experience of men and affairs. And
these had seemingly convinced him, once and for

all, that the pursuit of truth may be dearly pur-
chased, if the price for it is the clash of controversy
and the unsettlement of convictions. ' I will not,'
he writes in a significant passage, ' enter into the
question how much truth is preferable to peace.
Perhaps truth may be far better. But as we have
scarcely ever the same certainty in the one we have
in the other, I would—unless the truth were evident
indeed—hold fast to peace which has in her company
charity the highest of the virtues.' [1] The passage
might, on a first glance, seem to breathe the spirit
of toleration ; for does it not speak of charity ?
But in reality it tells in the opposite direction. For
when a man is ready to sacrifice truth to peace, he
is not likely to do justice to that assertion of freedom
to think, even at risk of atheism and infidelity,
which the pursuit of truth inexorably demands.

2. To this, however, we must add the further
point that the beliefs which the infidel and the
atheist denied were never viewed by Burke as
merely religious : they were always regarded as
politically indispensable. Rightly or wrongly, he
was wholly convinced that the institutions he most
valued, however strongly buttressed by authority,
prescription, and traditional loyalty, could not survive the disintegration of religious faith. The axe
was laid to the root of the tree from the moment
when political allegiance was divorced from those

[1] Speech, Feb. 6, 1772.

religious beliefs and sentiments which are of the essence of man as ' a religious animal.'

This is the ultimate ground of his intolerance. Convinced that the religious consciousness of a people could not be undetermined without shaking the foundations of the commonwealth, he was not content to urge that it was the duty of the states- man to foster religion by Church establishment and comprehensive toleration of all religious faiths. He went on, in an evil hour for his reputation for tolerance and charity, to erect the civil magistrate into the defender of the faith against infidels and atheists.   The best that can be said for him is that, within his limits, he was tolerant enough ; and it is a cheerful change to turn from these fulminations against freedom of thought to the declaration that all sorts of religion that exist within the State are to be tolerated because ' there is a reasonable worship in them all.' [1]

Even this catholic declaration, however, is to be understood with two reservations :—

(1) The first is that Burke was always peculiarly suspicious of any covert introduction of political propagandism under the mask of pleas and claims for religious liberty. Of this he furnishes significant proof.   In 1773 he had supported a Bill for the relief of Protestant dissenters.   He did this on the just and reasonable ground (among others) that it is bad

[1] Speech on Relief of Protestant Dissenters, 1773.

policy to make difficulties for conscientious and
honest dissenters which 'atheists' may only too easily
evade. 'These atheists,' he says, illustrating his
point from history, 'eluded all that you could do :
so will all free-thinkers for ever. Then you suffer,
or the weakness of your law has suffered, these great
dangerous animals to escape notice, whilst you have
nets that entangle the poor, fluttering, silken wings
of a tender conscience.' [1] But the scene changes.
In 1792 he opposes a similar petition from the Uni-
tarians ; not, however, because he had changed his
views on toleration, but because, rightly or wrongly,
he was convinced that the petition was, in its real
impelling motive, a political movement with political designs behind it. It was, in short, all too
closely linked with the militant radicalism and
radicals of whom he was the irreconcilable foe.
His line of argument is hardly convincing ; and a
critic might suggest that it is not less intolerable
that political hostility and conservative fears should
develop opposition to the relief of the religious
conscience than that the religious conscience should
become politically aggressive. But it is characteristic. Discerning in the Petition of 1792 a veiled
attack on the constitution, already menaced by
the spread of Jacobinism, and in particular on the
Church of England, to which the petitioners were
anything but friendly, he withstood it to the face,

[1] Speech on Relief of Protestant Dissenters, 1773.

as, on his own avowal, he never would have dreamt
of withstanding it, had he regarded it as nothing
more than a movement for the relief of aggrieved
consciences.

(2) The second reservation is that toleration
never meant for Burke, even in his most tolerant
mood, anything approaching to abstract religious
equality. He was ready, as we have seen, to tolerate
all religions ; he was willing to urge relief of Non-
conformist consciences ; he did not hesitate to
incur bitter odium, and even to sacrifice his seat,
by pleading, with an extraordinary persuasiveness,
for the relaxation of the penal laws that weighed
heavily on his Roman Catholic fellow-countrymen
in Ireland. But there he stopped. ' Dissent not
satisfied with toleration,' he once said, ' is not conscience but ambition.' [1] For it was, in his eyes,
ambition and not conscience that grudged the
Church of England as by law established either
her privileges, her national dignity, her endowments,
or (we must add) her tests.

To understand this, however, we must turn to
his well-known plea for the political value of religion, and for Church establishment in particular.

[1] Speech on the Acts of Uniformity, Feb. 1772.

CHAPTER VIII

RELIGION AND POLITICS

BURKE's political religion has its roots deep in three convictions. The first is that civil society rests on spiritual foundations, being indeed nothing less than a product of Divine will; the second, that this is a fact of significance so profound that the recognition of it is of vital moment, both for the corporate life of the State and for the lives of each and all of its members; and the third, that whilst all forms of religion within the nation may play their part in bearing witness to religion, this is peculiarly the function of an Established Church, in which the 'consecration of the State' finds its appropriate symbol, expression, and support.

On the first of these convictions it would be needless to enlarge. Enough to reinforce what has been already said by a single sentence which contains the sum of the whole matter : 'They '— he is speaking of both reflecting and unreflective men—'conceive that He who gave our nature to be perfected by our virtue, willed also the necessary means of its perfection. He willed therefore the State. He willed its connection with the

122

source and original archetype of all perfection.' [1]
It follows that the problem how to unite the secular
and the sacred in the life of the State, much as it
may perplex many minds, is not one that, in its
general aspect at any rate, troubles Burke.   As
the product of Divine will and of the ' stupendous
wisdom' that operates throughout the ages, the
State is in itself inherently and inalienably sacred.
It is not an institution, secular in its nature and
then made sacred by an ' alliance ' with a Church.
This is the very fallacy he rejects when touching
incidentally on the large and thorny topic of Church
and State: 'An alliance between Church and State
in a Christian commonwealth is, in my opinion, an
idle and a fanciful speculation.   An alliance is between two things that are in their nature distinct and
independent, such as between two sovereign States.
But in a Christian commonwealth, the Church and
the State are one and the same thing, being different
integral parts of the same whole.' [2]   And this
' whole,' this State in the larger and more comprehensive sense of the word, is always, in its entire
constitution, and not merely in its ecclesiastical
institutions, however important and august, the
result of that ' Divine tactic ' which presides over
the evolution of a nation.   It is needless, however,
to labour this point further.   For if civil society
does not rest on theistic and (we may add) on

[1] *Reflections.*   [2] Speech, May 11, 1792.

Christian foundations, if it be not vitalised through and through by the spirit of God, it must be evident by this time that Burke's political teaching is false precisely where he most passionately believed it to be true.

But if this be fact; if God, Providence, stupendous wisdom, Divine tactic, be of a verity thus operative in the growth and gradual organisation of civil society, it is not a matter to which the citizens of any State can afford to shut their eyes. On the contrary, its recognition by every citizen, small or great, is fraught with results of momentous significance. So, at least, Burke will have it. And if we grant his premises, his inference is unimpeachable. It is not credible that the citizens of any commonwealth can see the will of God in the history of their country, in the institutions under which they live, in the civic functions they discharge, in the ends to which they give their lives, without their attitude being influenced thereby. With the belief that ' God willed the State,' if it be indeed a real, and not a merely notional belief, there inevitably comes a reverent and dutiful, and even at times a quietistic spirit, such as can hardly be expected where the social system is regarded as begotten, sustained, and sanctioned by merely secular forces and a merely secular utility. For however true it may be—and happily there is no need to deny it—that even the most

secularly minded of citizens may love his country,
respect its laws, and if need be lay down his life for
it, there must always be a difference in political
motive between him and his genuinely religious-
minded neighbour. For, of course, political motive,
like all motive, reflects the nature of the object that
evokes it ; and, so long as this is so, it is idle to
suppose that the citizen who accepts his station and
its duties as prescribed by the supreme object of
human worship will not be profoundly influenced
thereby. As man and as citizen, he will most certainly be different; and there are no differences
between man and man that go deeper than differences
in constitution of motive.

But Burke goes much further than this. Not
only did he believe that religion makes a difference ;
he was convinced that it makes a better citizen.
And the peculiar interest of his writings here lies,
not in mere eloquent generalities, but in his specifi-
cation of the quite definite ways in which the
vitality of the religious spirit must influence the
citizen's outlook on the world of politics.

The difficulty of doing full justice to him here
is that the glowing sentences of his rhetoric lose
so much by translation into the cold and cut-and-
dried statements of abbreviated exposition. But,
per contra, it is just because critics are apt to think
eloquence is not argument, that it is important to
note how definite and how forcible are the reasons

which here, as in so many of Burke's pages, underlie the rhetoric. First and central is the bold assertion that it is only a religious consciousness that
can appreciate in its true significance the persistence and continuity of national life. This sounds
audacious. But on no point is Burke more insistent.
In one passage we have the affirmation that, were
the religious consciousness destroyed, 'no one
generation could link with another,' and 'men
become little better than the flies of a summer ' ; [1]
and in another the sweeping prediction that 'the
commonwealth itself would, in a few generations,
crumble away, be disconnected into the dust and
powder of individuality, and at length dispersed to
all the winds of heaven.' [2] Words can no further
go. If these be true, the conscious dependence of
the human on the Divine, and the continuity of a
nation's life stand and fall together.

Not that Burke was unaware that there are other
resources by which generation may be made to link
with generation. 'Prescriptive constitution,' 'entailed inheritance,' 'bank and capital of the ages,'
'experience of the species,' and other phrases of
like import, are all of them conceptions suggestive of ways in which political continuity may be
sustained and fostered. The point is that Burke,
though himself the prolific author of such phrases,
is convinced that more is needed. They may

[1] *Reflections.*   [2] *Ibid.*

suggest that the national life is a legacy : they do not, or at any rate not sufficiently, suggest that it is a supreme trust. They bear witness to the fact that a nation has a history : they do not enough convey the still more strengthening reminder that it has an assured leading and destiny, in the light of which its traditions and achievement gain an enhanced significance. For it is never enough for Burke that social organisms should be thrust forwards to an astonishing pitch of development by the mere *vis a tergo* of natural evolutionary forces, which, so far as evolutionists can tell, may quite possibly be fortuitous and aimless. He craves for more. To illuminate the struggles of the past, to dignify and intensify the responsibilities of the present, and to guarantee the future against the decadence and defeat with which, in a world of turbulent human wills, it is constantly menaced, it seemed to him the sheet anchor of a true political faith that the whole great drama of national life should be reverently recognised as ordered by a Power to which past, present, and future are organically knit stages in one Divine plan. ' There is an order that keeps things fast in their place ; it is made to us, and we are made to it,' [1] so runs his creed.

Results follow. For a belief such as this transfigures at a stroke the idea of the service of the

[1] Speech, May 7, 1782.

State ; and it does this, he tells us, especially in the case of ' persons of exalted station.' There is a paradox in Plato which declares that it is in vain to expect any man to be a great statesman unless he cares for something greater than politics. And though it may seem foolhardy to apply it to Burke, to whom politics were as the breath of his nostrils, it is none the less applicable. For both thinkers see the pitfalls that all too obviously lie in wait for the mere secular politician—the absorption in affairs, the greed for power, the sinister promptings of self-interest, the spirit of faction. And both would look for remedy in the same direction—in that purification of motive that springs from the elevation of the vocation of the statesman into nothing less than a ministry of the unseen. ' All persons possessing any portion of power,' so run the words, ' ought to be strongly and awfully impressed with an idea that they act in trust ; and that they are to account for their conduct in that trust to the one great Master, Author, and Founder of society.' [1] The words are in the very spirit of Plato, if we do but translate the language of a theistic faith into the reasoned terminology of Platonic metaphysics.

But it is not to ' persons of exalted station ' alone that this line of thought applies. In truth, it never applies with so much force and urgency as in democracies, where political power has been cut

[1] *Reflections.*

up into minute fragments and portioned out in wide
franchises. For it is just the wide distribution of
political power that may disastrously impair the
sense of individual responsibility. Burke has some
weighty sentences here. The people, he points
out, are, to a far less extent than are princes and
other persons of exalted station, 'under responsibility to one of the greatest controlling powers
on earth, the sense of fame and estimation. The
share of infamy that is likely to fall to the lot of
each individual in public acts is small indeed ; the
operation of opinion being in the inverse ratio to
the number of those who abuse power. Their own
approbation of their own acts has to them the appearance of a public judgment in their favour. A perfect democracy is therefore the most shameless thing
in the world. As it is the most shameless, it is also
the most fearless. No man apprehends in his person
he can be made subject to punishment. Certainly
the people at large never ought : for as all punish-
ments are for example towards the conservation of
the people at large, the people at large can never
become the subject of punishment by any human
hand.' [1]

Few will deny that in this passage Burke touches
with a sure hand one of the dangers of democracy.
It is so much easier for human nature to be eager to
share power than to take its share of responsibility

[1] *Reflections.*

in using it. Nor would it be difficult to point the moral by reference to the capriciousness, or the levity, or the indifference that is too often found in the democratic electorates which have come into being since Burke's day. The question with many is to find the remedy. And the remedy to which Burke would have us turn is characteristic. The only adequate safeguard against these dangers of popular power is to be found in the vitality of the religious spirit in the class or classes whose will is law. For that, and that alone, can bring the citizen to realise that, in the giving of vote or the duties of office, he is fulfilling what Burke does not hesitate to call a 'holy function.' The words, no doubt, must sound extravagant to secular minds, to whom politics altogether is nothing more than a matter of most mundane business, and very far indeed from being 'holy.' But they are not the less on that account significant of the civic importance of religion as understood by one of the greatest of all its exponents. Reverently religious in his own life, convinced by his diagnosis of human nature that man is ' a religious animal,' and insistent always that religious institutions are an organic element in the body-politic, it was inevitable that Burke should recoil from a merely secular citizenship as unequal to the demands and burdens which the State imposes on its members. Secular minds may reject his teaching. To them it can only seem

a devout imagination. But they can be in no
doubt, if they have read his pages, that to leave
this aspect out would make his political message a
wholly different, and, in his eyes, an impoverished
thing.

Nor, perhaps, is it rash to assume that the vast
majority of the religious world would be in substantial sympathy with Burke's insistence on the
political value of religion, so far at any rate as we
have considered it. Presumably all religious organisations, including such as are frankly, and even
bitterly, hostile to established Churches, unite in
the aspiration that the religious spirit may permeate
life, of which political life is not the least part, from
end to end. Even those who protest that politics
ought to be kept separate from religion, and religion
from politics, must be aware, no matter how sharply
they distinguish secular and religious organisations
and their work, that they carry their religion with
them in the constitution of their motives, as these
operate in the performance of all important work
done by them for the world. That any citizen
should be religious, and that he should *not* be influenced thereby in motive, even in the most secular
of transactions, can only mean that in certain
departments of life he is not religious. Fullness of
life, and of strife, may have made the Churches
many, yet one must do them the justice of supposing that they all alike desire to leaven the

entire social system with Christian conscience and
Christian charity. And if this be so, they can
hardly fail to sympathise with the spirit of Burke's
teaching as a plea for the alliance of citizenship and
religion.

Burke, however, as is well known, would have his
readers go a step further. Neither the sanctuaries
of the heart nor the sanctuaries of voluntary Churches
are enough for him. For, as he found the Church
of England in possession of its prescriptive inheritance, material and spiritual, he insists, with all the
argument and eloquence in his resourceful treasury,
that it ought to stand as a recognition of religion
by the nation in its corporate capacity. Convinced,
as we have seen, that civil society as an organic
whole is a sacred institution, he pled for a national
and visible recognition of that fact. The ' corporate fealty and homage ' of the State to religion was
to him simply the public acknowledgment that
' God willed the State.' And this general principle
was backed by arguments as definite as they are
forcible.

One is the claim, which controversy has made
familiar, that religion—and not least because of the
intimacy of its connection with education—is too
momentous a national interest to be left to what he
calls ' the unsteady and precarious contribution of
individuals.'

Another is the plea that the clergy of an estab-

lished Church occupy a position which effectively
strengthens their hands as upholders of morality
and moral valuations. Not only can they bring
the consolations of religion to the hapless and
heavily burdened poor ; not only can they minister,
no less, to ' the distresses of the miserable great ' ;
they can also, from a position of independence,
such as he thinks is not enjoyed by a clergy directly
dependent on popular support, instruct ' pre-
sumptuous ignorance ' and rebuke ' insolent vice,'
whether in high estate or low. ' The people of
England,' he declares, ' will not suffer the insolence
of wealth and titles, or any other species of proud
pretension, to look down with scorn upon what they
look up to with reverence ; nor presume to trample
on that acquired personal nobility which they in-
tend always to be, and which often is, the fruit,
not the reward (for what can be the reward ?) of
learning, piety, and virtue.' [1] And it is but an
extension of this democratic demand for an independent aristocracy of the spirit that leads him
on to welcome the ' modest splendour and un-
assuming state, the mild majesty and sober pomp '
of religious ceremonial, and to justify an ecclesiastical hierarchy such as may (to quote a phrase
that has become familiar) ' exalt its mitred front
in courts and parliaments.'

A third point is that it is when a clergy enjoys

[1] *Reflections.*

the recognised position, and the financial independence which the establishment of religion
gives, that they are best placed to resist all temp-
tations to yield to tyrannical pressure either from
above or from below, and, by consequence, peculiarly
well fitted to stand for a genuine political liberty.
'The English,' he says, 'tremble for their liberty
from the influence of a clergy dependent on the
Crown ; they tremble for the public tranquillity
from the disorders of a factious clergy, if it were
made to depend upon any other than the Crown.
They therefore made their Church, like their king
and their nobility, independent.' [1]

Nor, finally, could he regard it as other than a
good application of public money, and not least
in the interests of the poorer classes, that it should
be devoted to religious purposes. He puts the
point with unqualified directness : 'For those
purposes they (*i.e.* those who believe that God
willed the State) think some part of the wealth
of the country is as usefully employed as it can
be in fomenting the luxury of individuals. It is
the public ornament. It is the public consolation.
It nourishes the public hope. The poorest man
finds his own importance and dignity in it, whilst
the wealth and pride of individuals at every moment
makes the man of humble rank and fortune sensible
of his inferiority, and degrades and vilifies his con-

[1] *Reflections.*

dition. It is for the man in humble life, and to
raise his nature, and to put him in mind of a
state in which the privileges of opulence will cease,
when he will be equal by nature, and may be more
than equal by virtue, that this portion of the
general wealth of his country is employed and
sanctified.' [1]

Nor does it in the least shake him in this that
the Church, thus supported by the general wealth,
should have its own tenets and tests, and that
these should exclude the conscientious noncon-
formist. Invoking the Lockian principle, which
no one is likely to dispute, that a voluntary society
can exclude any member she thinks fit on such
conditions as she thinks proper, he transfers the
principle, with a surprising indifference to the
significance of the transition, to the Church that
claims to be national.[2] It is precisely on this
ground, indeed, that he argues, in 1772, against
the petition, in which not only certain of the clergy
of the Church, but doctors and lawyers, claimed to
be relieved from subscription to the Articles. And
the line he took here is all the more remarkable,
because he was far from thinking that the Church
was perfect. Both Articles and Liturgy, he frankly
admits, are 'not without the marks and characters
of human frailty.' [3] This was, of course, to be

[1] *Reflections*.   [2] Speech on the Acts of Uniformity.
[3] *Ibid.*

lamented; but it was not enough to precipitate a change. Against a change he urges that there is no real grievance—none for the petitioning clergy, who may easily find pulpits and congregations to suit their views in one or other of the many Churches that are tolerated ; and none for the taxpayer, who, if he be one of a minority who dissent from the creed of the Church, is not to be supposed to subscribe to the creed because he consents to pay his tax. Nor has he much difficulty in showing that, in suggesting subscription to Scripture as substitute, the petitioners were opening up as many difficulties as those they wished to escape. *Some* test of membership, he insists, every Church must impose ; men must not expect to be paid by taxation ' for teaching, as Divine truths, their own particular fancies.' And this being so, he would rather have subscription to the Articles, with all their imperfections, than anything that can be put in their place.

There is much in this that will no doubt invite criticism in days when both Church establishment and Creed subscription are more burning questions than they were then. But it is not necessary to embark here on either of these highly controversial topics. Enough if what has been said makes it clear how far Burke carried his repugnance to anything that savoured of the secularisation of the State.

For it is not Burke's defence of Church establishment that is the central interest in his apologia for
religion in politics ; it is rather the grounds on
which this rests—grounds which will appeal to
many besides those who stand for established
religions. Is it true that the belief that God has
willed the State is fraught for citizens with these
momentous issues which Burke ascribes to it ? Is
it a fact that the State is a sacred thing ? Is it
incontrovertible that the trite distinction between
secular and sacred is a pernicious and false dualism ?
Is it the case that religion is the basis of civil society ?
These are questions that go deeper far than the vexed
controversy about Church establishments. For it
is not the adherents of established Churches alone,
it is the whole religious world that finds itself nowadays in the presence of critics and assailants more
numerous, more formidable, more scientific than
the atheists and infidels of Burke's abhorrence and
denunciation. For the nineteenth century has
seen the advent, not to say—for not a few would say
it—the triumph, of naturalism. And in political
theory naturalism, of course, means not only that
the social organism, like other organisms, comes to
its maturity through the action of biological laws,
but that the prolonged process of struggle and sur-
vival through which it emerges, finds all the explanation available in the operation of quite secular
conditions and causes, possibly in the last resort

mechanical, but at any rate such as leave no room
for the agency of any final cause or providential
agency whatsoever. Nor is it doubtful that any
such notion as that the course of history and the
evolution of nations are ' the known march of the
providence of God,' would receive but a chilling
welcome at the hands of naturalism. If so, the
practical inference is obvious. Ill would it become
the statesman to cherish one thought, or utter one
word, about a ' Divine tactic,' ' a stupendous wisdom,' a ' Divine Disposer,' or what not. Let the
will of evolution be done ! Enough for him to be
content, as the naturalistic thinkers are content, to
learn from experience what the facts and forces are
that are thrusting on his country he knows not
whither. Enough for him to shape these facts and
control these forces in the interests of the public
good, or whatever other end he can find, and sufficiently believe in, to vitalise the civic will to strenuous service. Nor presumably would either theoretical or practical naturalism resent the imputation that it leads to a thoroughgoing secularisation
of the State.

Nor can it be denied that it would be in vain to
seek for a refutation of naturalism in the pages of
Burke. He does not prove, he never dreams of
proving that man is a religious animal, or that the
object of religious faith is real. His religion is a
faith, not a philosophy ; and those who wish to find

these fundamentals of the faith made good by proof, must go, not to Burke but to the theologians, or to the idealistic philosophers who are not afraid to give the world a philosophy of religion. And yet Burke's teaching has its claims upon the thinker. It suggests a problem which is theoretically, as well as practically, of the first rank. For, by the passionate conviction and definiteness of statement wherewith he specifies the ways in which the vitality of the religious consciousness influences the attitude of the citizen of all ranks and grades towards his station and its duties—a matter on which he could speak with the voice of experience—he prompts the question as to what is likely to happen should religious belief suffer eclipse. Will that consciousness of imperious political obligation, which so often has had its root in theism, survive ? Will the faith that men and nations have a destiny no less assured and divinely guided than their past history, still play its part in fostering that belief in ideals in which lies the nerve of political struggle ? Will an unselfish devotion to the public good still persist ? Hardly can it be denied that hitherto the resolute and dutiful civic spirit has thriven, not only in illustrious instances, but amongst masses of the people, in close alliance with religion. To quicken and sustain it, more has seemingly been needed than the consciousness of ties to home, to comrades, to neighbourhood, to nation, to humanity. The appeal to altar has been as potent as to hearth. ' It is in the form of imagination,' says a writer on political obligation, who never ventured on a statement till he felt that his foot was planted on experience,[1] ' the imagination of a supreme, invisible, but all-seeing ruler that, in the case at least of all ordinary good people, the idea of an absolute duty is so brought to bear upon the soul as to yield an awe superior to any personal inclination.' If this be true, how is the gap to be filled should this article of practical faith become in the eyes of ' all ordinary good people,' as doubtless it already is to naturalistic scrutiny, no better than an imaginative figment best relegated to the scrap-heap of past, or passing, phases of metaphysical illusion ? For the strength and vitality of motives depends ultimately upon the objects to which they attach themselves, and by which they are fed and fostered. And so long as this is so, it would seem something of a venture to remove a God, a 'Divine Disposer,' a 'Providence,' a 'Divine tactic,' from the human horizon without finding some substitute.

This, indeed, seems to be well recognised, for naturalistic minds do not revolt against political theism without putting something in the place of the deity deposed and the ' Divine tactic ' superseded. Sometimes it is the Nation which, following a French lead, they set on the secular altar of civic

[1] Professor T. H. Green.

devotion.[1] And sometimes, and not by any means
only amongst avowed positivists, it is Humanity.
Nor is it to be doubted that both are great and
enduring objects to which the minds and hearts
of men will never look in vain for incentive and
support.

This, however, is not a statement that Burke of
all men would have been likely to challenge. There
is abundant room in his scheme of life, as we have
already seen,[2] both for the nation and humanity.
No writer in our language, or in any language, is
less open to the charge of underestimating the
strength of the patriotic motive. To this we need
not return. But then it has to be remembered
that it was not the nation as a merely secular institution that aroused this passion of patriotism, but
the nation consecrated in his imagination as product
and instrument of the Divine will. It is not worth
asking whether his patriotism would have survived
the destruction of his theism, because in his mind
the two things are one and indivisible.

Similarly with the larger, though far less closely
knit, object, humanity. Burke was not blind to
it. Despite his denunciations of French fraternity,
he never failed, as we have seen,[3] to recognise that
his own country, and all countries, were parts of a
larger whole. But this larger whole was not the

---

[1] *E.g.* Pearson in *National Life and Character.*
[2] P. 23 *et seq.*   [3] P. 27.

humanity of positivism or naturalism; it was
' the great mysterious incorporation of the human
race '; and the mystery that encompassed it was
not the mystery that, to the agnostic, shuts out the
faith that the fortunes of the race are shaped and
controlled by spiritual forces, but the mystery which,
however dark and inscrutable (the words are his
own), is still compatible with the belief that the
course of civilisation is ' the known march of the
ordinary providence of God.' Certainly for the
mind of Burke there could be no ultimate rest
in the idea of humanity. How could there be,
when it was to him of the essence of humanity,
by the perennial vitality of the religious consciousness, to bear its witness to the dependence
of the human on the Divine ? It needs no words
to prove that if man be ' a religious animal,' if
atheism be against both human instincts and
human reason, as Burke declared it was, ' humanity ' was ill fitted to be offered to the world
as a *substitute* for God. For, though it may need
few words to prove that, if humanity be severed
by the sword of science from divinity, and God
left out as but an ancient idol, the apotheosis of
humanity is the deposition of divinity; it is not
less obvious that the idea of a humanity, in
every individual soul of which the belief in God
is eternal and ineradicable, is the strongest of
all securities against the secularisation of human

life. Yet nothing less than this was the creed of
Burke, to whose profoundly religious spirit the
attempted secularisation of history and politics was
nothing less than a conspiracy to denationalise the
nation and to dehumanise the race.

CHAPTER IX

GOVERNMENT

FIERCE and inveterate as is Burke's hostility to the revolutionists, there is one cardinal point upon which he and they are at one. Both he and they believe that, behind the struggles and the flux of politics, there is an objective order which (to revert once more to Burke's words) holds all things fast in their place, and that to this objective order men and nations are bound to adapt themselves. 'It is made to us, and we are made to it.'

For the radical thinkers of that day were neither unbelievers nor utilitarians, but dogmatists. They dogmatised the natural rights of man, in which they saw an order of things, not made by man and never to be destroyed by man, to which all politics were bound, sooner or later, and sooner rather than later, to conform. Nor was this faith shaken ; it was only put to the proof by the fact that, in all existing states—except the new American republic and the still newer French experiment—these eternal rights were ignored and outraged. So much the worse for existing states. It followed from this that, when these radicals came to theorise on government,

144

they laid its foundations in the rights of man inalien-
able, imprescriptible, not to be questioned by the
sons of men. This was the one way of political
salvation. For whatever government could or
could not do, it remained its paramount function
to enact and uphold natural rights, with as firm a
faith as though they were the ordinances of the
Most High, which indeed to many, to Price, for
example, or Paine, they were.

From this dogmatism, however, Burke (as must
be by this time evident) dissented, and his words
are direct and explicit : ' The foundation of government is there '—he is speaking of the *Reflections*—
' laid, not in imaginary rights of men (which at best
is a confusion of judicial with civil principles), but
in political convenience, and in human nature ;
either as that nature is universal, or as it is modified by local habits and social aptitudes. The
foundation of government (those who have read
that book will recollect) is laid in a provision for
our wants, and in a conformity to our duties ; it
is to purvey for the one ; it is to enforce the
other.' [1]

Nor does the interest of this passage lie only in its
refusal to build on the ' imaginary ' foundation of
natural rights. Obviously, in its appeal to ' political convenience ' and ' human nature,' it is well
fitted to carry the suggestion that the writer of it

[1] *Appeal.*

had repudiated the false foundation of rights only to adopt the foundation of utility. And, *in a sense*, this is true. We have already seen the stress Burke lays upon the happiness of the whole people as the paramount end of all political endeavour. So much so, that it might easily appear as if, here in his handling of government, he had simply, like any Benthamite, taken his stand on expediency, and, equally like any Benthamite, quite lost sight of what the utilitarians would probably have called the ' transcendental ' foundations of his political creed as these stand written in his political religion. This, however, is far from the fact. The foundation of government is not laid in utility. And this will quickly become evident, if we revert to his attitude to the dogmatists of natural rights. For in holding to his political theism, with a faith so passionate that it drove him to urge the persecution of atheists and infidels, he never laid claim to any immediate revelation of the eternal laws of justice and reason at all comparable to that which was so confidently written in the cut-and-dried codes of the rights of man. He was more modestly content to interpret the will of God as written in the gradual revelation of his country's history. However firmly he believed in a divinely ordained objective order that holds all things fixed in their place, he never dreamed of dogmatising *a priori* as to what this objective order is or prescribes.

The very attempt was hateful in his eyes. He preferred to consult experience as unfolded in that long and gradual process of historical evolution in which, as he believed, the dispositions of a stupendous wisdom were to be discerned. This was for him the one way of sober thought and sound statesmanship. To take the other path, to dogmatise abstract codes of rights as if they were a direct revelation from Heaven, and then to proceed to realise them forthwith as if history and experience had nothing to reveal—this was the way of fanatics.

But if this divides Burke from the revolutionists, it also divides him from the utilitarians. For it has always been what some folk think the strength, and others the weakness, of Benthamism that, repudiating the uncongenial alliance of Paley, it stood for a political philosophy that was unmitigatedly secular. It has ever fought shy (to say the least) of metaphysics. And though in J. S. Mill (who was after all a kind of heretic from its faith) it began to do justice to the past, it was never much concerned to interpret either past, present, or future in the light of a larger and more cosmic philosophy. On the contrary, having discovered what it mistook for bed-rock in its ideal of a Greatest Happiness of a Greatest Number, it was well content to build on that and to sink no deeper shaft. It was reserved for the younger Mill to try to prove—and with

indifferent success—the Benthamite position.   And
it is, of course, on that position that their theory of
government, and much else besides, stands or falls.
It is here that Burke parts company from them.
We have seen that, in a sense, he was utilitarian—in
the sense that the happiness of the people was
always his paramount practical end, as it was
theirs.[1]   But we have seen also that his conception
of a people was not theirs.[2]   Their conception was
arithmetical ; his was biological : their conception
was that of an aggregate of units working for the
happiness of the largest possible sum of units ; his
was that of an organic whole : their conception
that of a community in which ' each was to count
for one,' and where the value of the units was to
be estimated by nothing but susceptibilities to
pleasures and pains ; his was that of an inequali-
tarian partnership in which the value of the units
varies through many degrees according to the
station, functions and capacities which are assigned
to the inevitably unequal members of every civil
society by ' the discipline of nature ' : theirs, in
short, was the conception of a society which recognised no higher law than the dictates of expediency
construed in the light of a hedonistic psychology ;
his of a society in which the appeal to political
convenience and human nature was sufficiently
strong to constrain the human will only when it

[1] P. 45.   [2] P. 56.

was understood as carrying in it a deeper reference
to the Divine government of the world.

If therefore it be said—and it is certainly true—
that the end of all government for Burke, as for
Bentham, is the happiness of the people, this admission must find room for these vital differences. For
in Burke's eyes it is no part of the end of government,
because it is wholly at variance with what a people
is, that the inequalities between class and class or
man and man, should be reduced to a minimum.
The point he singles out for special admiration in
the philosophers of antiquity is the care they bestowed in discriminating the various classes or
orders of which a state consists. And it is but the
same thing from the other side that, of all the
larger ideas that move the political world, equality
appeals to him the least. Political equality and
social equality were alike illusions and fictions.
He was content instead with that moral equality,
that ' true moral equality of mankind ' as he calls
it, which is within the reach of all classes, because it
depends neither on franchises nor wealth nor rank,
but on the happiness that is to be found by virtue
in all conditions. And though he stood firm, no
man firmer, for equality of civil rights, it was in
the conviction that these were the just and necessary conditions on which the endlessly varied inequalities of capacity, opportunity, and achievement were certain to emerge. The *interests* of the

people were always paramount, and the interests
of the poor were second to none ; but these interests
were never so safe as in a social system which
perpetuated class distinctions, and, we may add,
never so much imperilled as in a society of levellers.
Burke could indeed come to no other conclusion.
It followed from his principles. Grant that the
people means the organised people ; grant that the
organisation of a people, in the only true sense of
that all-important word, comes by the gradual
evolution of a nation's life ; grant that the course
of the evolution, ' the discipline of nature,' is a
sifting process through which a society comes to
be differentiated into varied ranks, classes, orders,
vocations, interests ; grant, finally, that this great
historical drama is religiously accepted as ' the
march of the ordinary providence of God '—what
else can befit the statesman who holds to the happiness of the people as the supreme end of government
than to do his best to perpetuate class distinctions
rather than to demolish them ; especially if he be
convinced that the march of the levellers leads
straight to misery and ruin ?

This may prepare the way for the further question :
In what hands, then, is the trust of power to be
reposed ? And for the answer that the organ of
government is a hereditary monarch, a hereditary
peerage and aristocracy, and a representative

chamber holding its tenure by the votes of an exceedingly select electorate. This was the political constitution Burke found at work ; he thought it had worked admirably well, so well that he set himself to defend it against all comers with a resource and eloquence which have made him, in this aspect, by far the greatest of all conservatives.

Not that he is to be classed, not by any means, amongst the worshippers of kings. He looked up to kings, he would have all men look up to them ' with awe.' He clothed them with that dignity which all that was ancient and august always wore to his historic imagination. And he was far from wishing to strip them of real power, and least of all as intermediaries of foreign policy, admirably fitted to prevent pernicious foreign intrigue with political factions.[1] He was convinced that monarchy was the best of all governments. But he was none the less minded to keep kings in their place. Not only did he brush contemptuously aside those ' old exploded fanatics of slavery,' the apologists of Divine right ; he spent the years of his prime (as we have seen) in resisting, with infinite resource of reasoning and rhetoric, the insidious revival of royal prerogative in the hateful form of corrupt Georgian influence. Few factions in the State have ever had to stand so merciless a fire as ' the king's friends' of those fighting years. Nor would it be true

[1] *Reflections.* Cf. *Observations on the Conduct of the Minority.*

to say of Burke, except perhaps in his chivalrous
and pathetic tribute to hapless Marie Antoinette,
that the throne was invested with that glamour
which it wore to the romantic imagination of Scott.
There was a practicality about him that prevented
it.   Indeed, we even find the startlingly unflattering
remark that ' kings are naturally lovers of low
company,' [1] with the still more unflattering inference that they need a dignified and well-paid, even
if idle, court aristocracy to stand between them
and their possible ' flatterers, tale-bearers, para-
sites, pimps, and buffoons.'   His case for monarchy
is, in fact, historic and practical, rather than senti-
mental and romantic.   It rests on the conviction
that a hereditary king has been, is, and ought to
continue to be, an essential element in the prescriptive constitution, ' the keystone that binds
together the noble and well-constructed arch of our
empire and our constitution,' [2] and on the generalisation, for which surely there is much to be said,
that, even granting—for he concedes so much—
that a republic might, in rare cases, be justifiable;[3]
it ought ever to be borne in mind that—as Boling-
broke had remarked—it is always easier to graft
democratic elements on monarchy than any
monarchical element on democracy.

On this ground he takes his stand with a firm-

[1] Speech on the Economical Reform.
[2] Speech at Bristol, November 3, 1774.
[3] *Reflections.*

ness and a combativeness that know no faltering.
If, in a sense, a king may be called ' the servant of
the people,' it is only in a sense.[1] Emphatically
' servant ' is not the word, if it be taken to suggest
that like a menial he obeys the commands of a
master, and were removable at pleasure. The
King of England at any rate holds by another
tenure. He is ' a real king and not an executive
officer.' [2] As such his power is, and ought to be,
equally real. ' The direct power of the King of
England,' he writes (in 1791), ' is considerable. His
indirect and far more certain power is great indeed.
He stands in need of nothing towards dignity ; of
nothing towards splendour ; of nothing towards
authority ; of nothing at all towards consideration
abroad.' [3] Indeed, it was just because he knew
how great could be the real power of a Crown
that is hereditary, personally irresponsible, and
firmly established since 1688 as ' the keystone of
the constitution,' that he declared, in one of his
latest writings, that ' jealousy of the Crown ' is an
inherent principle of the British constitution—a
principle, he adds, which must be kept ' eternally
and chastely burning.' [4] No one did more to keep
that flame alight than Burke. But this never
touched his convinced acceptance of the principle

[1] *Reflections.*
[2] Letter to a Member of the National Assembly.
[3] *Ibid.*
[4] *Regicide Peace*, Letter IV.

that the king holds his place of dignity and power, not indeed in defiance of his people—for had not the people in 1688 interfered with the succession ? —but, still, independently of them, inasmuch as his tenure is indubitably hereditary, and such as could only by a gross abuse of words and facts be described as dependent on the *choice* of his subjects. To argument he adds derision, to derision contempt, and to contempt invective, in his zeal to convict Dr. Richard Price and the other ' gentlemen of the society for revolutions ' of talking a ' confused jargon ' ; because, though ' they had not a vote for a king amongst them,' they made bold to claim the right ' to choose their own governors,' and ' to cashier them for misconduct.' Whether the constitutional history that lay behind his diatribes against Price and his following was sound is a question on which we need not enter. He was aware himself that he was writing as combatant, as advocate, rather than as judge. Enough that the controversy makes it sufficiently clear that the Whig respect for government by consent never brought him within measurable distance of the damnable heresy that the Crown was, or ought to be, elective. It is an interesting exercise for students of Constitutional Law to follow the pleadings of his arguments, perhaps not quite convincing, that 1688 was a revolution ' not made but prevented,' and that the substitution of William for James was

carefully carried through as a necessary deviation
which was never meant to be the basis of a general
principle.[1]

The same whole-hearted acceptance of the hereditary principle appears, as might be expected, in his
many pleas for an aristocracy of birth, possessions,
and privilege. For not only was an hereditary nobility (as we have all read) ' the Corinthian capital of
polished society,' it was a symbol of permanence, and,
like a church establishment, one of the best securities
for continuity and stability in a nation's life, ' the
chain that connects the ages of a nation.' The power
of perpetuating property in a family, by primo-
geniture or otherwise, was just one of those ways
in which private ambitions may become tributary
to public good. The assailants of landed property
and inheritance were the worst enemies of the State.
He calls them the worst enemies of the poor. Nor
did he think it in the smallest degree a sacrifice of
liberty, or any contradiction to government by
consent, that social rank and aristocratic connection and broad acres should enjoy a favoured
position in political power. Only envy and little-
ness of mind would grudge it to them.

Of this he gives a striking proof. When the
Whig party at last came into brief tenure of power
it does not seem to have so much as crossed his

[1] See *Reflections* and *Appeal*.

mind that it was other than in the nature of things
that he, who had given up to his party what was
meant for mankind, should be excluded from the
Cabinet. The modesty, the humility of his words
is astonishing : ' I am not a man so foolishly vain,
nor so blindly ignorant of my own state and condition, as to indulge for a moment the idea of my
becoming a minister.' [1] There was no affectation
here, and subserviency is not a word to be coupled
with the name of Burke. For his relations with
the nobility were, in the main, those of business.
He did not covet their society. He had no appetite
for the life of courts, or of fashion, and not much
for the pageantries of public ceremonial. He preferred Johnson and Garrick and his friends and
comrades at the club, and the quiet life of his home,
and his cheerful intercourse there with his work-folk
amongst the tilth and pastures of Beaconsfield. And
his estimates were in keeping with his life. ' I
am no friend to aristocracy,' he once said, ' in the
sense at least in which that word is usually understood. If it were not a bad habit to moot cases
on the supposed ruin of the constitution, I should
be free to declare that, if it must perish, I would
rather by far see it resolved in any other form than
lost in that austere and insolent domination.' [2]
It is not an isolated utterance. When many years

---

[1] MacKnight's *Life*, vol. ii. p. 488.
[2] *Thoughts on the Present Discontents.*

had gone by, he repeated the same thing in even stronger phrase : 'I am accused of being a man of aristocratic principles. If by aristocracy they mean the peers, I have no vulgar admiration, nor any vulgar antipathy, towards them ; I hold their order in cold and decent respect. I hold them to be of absolute necessity in the constitution, but I think they are only good when kept within their proper bounds.' [1]

Nor can there be any doubt at all that for what Carlyle called ' a gracefully going idle in Mayfair aristocracy,' he had in full measure the strenuous worker's withering contempt. In his *Letter to a Noble Lord* he said some stinging things which must have gone home to many another besides the raw and inexperienced aristocrat against whom they were levelled. 'Whatever his (the Duke of Bedford's) natural parts may be, I cannot recognise in his few and idle years the competence to judge of my long and laborious life. . . . Poor rich man ! He can hardly know anything of public industry in its exertions, or can estimate its compensations when its work is done.' 'I was not,' he adds, ' like his Grace of Bedford, swaddled and rocked and dandled into a legislator.'

For it is here as elsewhere. Burke looked on aristocracy primarily with the eye of the man of affairs. Much as he respected old families and

[1] Speech on Repeal of the Marriage Acts, 1781.

many of their living representatives ; eloquently
as he has written of pedigrees and illustrating ancestors, of bearings and ensigns armorial, of galleries
of portraits, monumental inscriptions, records,
evidences and titles ; and though it had been a
hope—pathetic in its frustration—' to be in some
fashion the founder of a family,' it was not on
these things that his settled estimates and sentiments really rested. They had other and more
solid grounds. As he read history, aristocratic influence had done great things for England ; and
he preferred, as he was wont to prefer, the performance of the constitution to the untried substitutes of theorising levellers ; he realised that aristocratic connection was an immense actual force in
the politics of the present ; he regarded landed
property as ' the firm base of every stable government ' ; [1] and he held it a sound principle that
large masses of property in few hands needed for
its security a correspondingly larger share in political power ; not least, he was convinced that inherited rank and inherited acres and their con-
comitants opened up for their fortunate possessors
opportunities for dealing with affairs upon a large
scale which, if rightly used, would prove perhaps
the best of all preparatives for the work of public
administration. That aristocracies have their defects he was well aware. He was not blind. No

[1] *Regicide Peace*, Letter III.

one saw with clearer vision the idleness, indifference,
self-seeking, arrogance, incapacity, and vice which
in many an instance defaced 'the Corinthian
capital of polished society.' 'The fat stupidity
and gross ignorance concerning what imports
men most to know which prevails at courts' is
not a flattering phrase. But these things—and
there were aristocrats before his eyes whose reputation was quite as spotted as that of John
Wilkes—never shook his political estimate of the
class, nor gave pause to the suggestion that it
augurs some defect of character to grudge to it its
dignity, advantages, and influence.

Nowhere, indeed, does this appear with greater
clearness than in the sentences where he is urging
the claims, not of rank but of ability and virtue, to
place and honour : ' You do not imagine that I wish
to confine power, authority, and distinction to blood
and names and titles. No, sir. There is no qualification for government but virtue and wisdom,
actual or presumptive. Wherever they are actually
found, they have, in whatever state, condition,
profession or trade, the passport of Heaven to
human place and honour.' [1] This is sweeping. But
we are not permitted to find in it, as we might expect, and most of all as coming from ' an Irish
adventurer,' a protest against the Whig exclusiveness which shut out this greatest of Whigs, this

[1] *Reflections.*

'John Wesley of politics,' from more than subordinate office.[1] The inference Burke draws follows a contrary direction. The ordeal which all but broke him down is not resented as a grievance. Rather is it welcomed as a touchstone by which it is good that, in all ages, the statesman should prove his quality. 'I do not hesitate to say,' so runs this most eloquent and least envious of all apologies for social disadvantages, 'that the road to eminence and power from obscure condition ought not to be made too easy, nor a thing too much of course. . . . The temple of honour ought to be seated on an eminence. If it be opened through virtue, let it be remembered that virtue is never tried but by some difficulty and some struggle.'[2] Who will deny that the words and the thought are noble ? Who can doubt that they are much nobler and more generous than the monopolistic spirit of aristocratic Whig exclusiveness, which we are not bound to resent the less in its treatment of Burke, because Burke did not resent it at all.

Burke's plea for an aristocracy of birth is however not to be fully understood without two further considerations : he never feared aristocracy, and he did fear democracy. For he could see no signs that the aristocracy—the genuine as distinguished from the backstairs aristocracy—was likely to menace the Crown. Nor did he think they had it in

---

[1] Paymaster of the Forces.   [2] *Reflections.*

them to be a menace to the people. 'Would to God!' he once exclaimed, 'that it were true that our peers have too much spirit.' And in accordance with the aspiration, the effort of his life was rather to adjure the nobility to stand in and do their duty to the State than to stir men's fears of aristocratic usurpation. His apprehensions were of a different kind. First he feared the Crown, the Crown that, in the person of George III., was so determined not only to reign but to govern ; and, when that fear was allayed, there followed that mixture of fear and fury with which he regarded the rising spectre of a revolutionary radicalism.

To understand this, however, we must turn to his views on representation and electorates.

Burke's statements about the place and importance of the people in government are so many and emphatic, that the hasty reader might think him far more democratic than he is. Here are some of them : 'If any ask me what a free government is, I answer that, for any practical purpose, it is what the people think so ; and that they, and not I, are the natural, lawful, and competent judges of this matter.' [1]

' There is no such thing as governing a people contrary to their inclinations. They are not votes and resolutions, they are not arms that govern a people.' [2]

' The people are the masters.' [3]

[1] Letter to the Sheriffs.   [2] MacKnight's *Life*, i. 305.
[3] Speech on the Economical Reform.

' The forms of government, and the persons who administer it, all originate from the people.' [1]

' The general opinion of those who are to be governed . . . is the vehicle and organ of legislative omnipotence.' [2]

' The desires of the people, when they do not militate with the stable and eternal rules of justice and reason (rules which are above us and above them),'— a significant qualification of which more hereafter— ' ought to be as a law to a House of Commons.' [3]

' The people may be deceived in their choice of an object. But I can hardly conceive any choice they can make to be so very mischievous as the existence of any human force capable of resisting it.' [4]

' Let us give a faithful pledge to the people that we honour, indeed, the Crown ; but that we *belong* to them ; that we are their auxiliaries, and not their task-masters ; the fellow-labourers in the same vineyard, not lording over their rights, but helpers of their joy.' [5]

Nor would it be in the least difficult to reinforce these passages by others, especially if we drew them from the days when he was rallying the Whigs to resist the Crown and ' the king's friends,' or when he was telling the House that it had neither

[1] *Thoughts on the Present Discontents.*
[2] Letter to the Sheriffs.   [3] *Economical Reform.*
[4] Letter on the Duration of Parliaments.
[5] *Economical Reform.*

right nor reason on its side in flouting John Wilkes and the electors of Middlesex.

Yet these utterances are not really democratic. For, in the first place, by the voice of ' the people,' he means the voice not of the majority but of the organised people—the people in his own sense of the term, as sifted by ' the discipline of nature,' not only (as already said) into many ranks, classes, and interests, but into many grades of political capacity—and incapacity. And as the area of political incapacity is wide in the extreme, the inference he would have us draw is that the electorate, if it is to reflect the people (truly so-called), must be exceedingly select—a mere handful, indeed, if we compare it with the millions who have come into power under a democratic franchise. Some words of his own reveal how very select on his idea of it, was not only the electorate, but the effective political public altogether. They show conclusively how far removed was the conservative Whig of the eighteenth century from the reforming Whig of the nineteenth, and still more from the twentieth-century Radical. ' I have often endeavoured to compute and to class those who, in any political view, are to be called the people. . . . In England and Scotland I compute that those of adult age, not declining in life, of tolerable leisure for such (*i.e.* political) discussions, and of some means of information, more or less, and who are above menial depen-

dence (or what virtually is such) may amount to
about four hundred thousand. There is such a
thing as a natural representative of the people.
This body is that representative ; and on this body,
more than on the legal constituent, the artificial
representative depends. This is the British public ;
and it is a public very numerous. The rest, when
feeble, are the objects of protection ; when strong,
the means of force.'[1]

With this state of things he was content.   He
says so : ' If there is a doubt whether the House of
Commons represents perfectly the whole commons
of Great Britain (I think there is none), there can
be no question but that the Lords and Commons
together represent the sense of the whole people to the
Crown and to the world.'[2]   It is clear that Burke's
version of government by 'the people' is far removed
from popular government, commonly so-called.

Hence his lifelong resistance to any popularisa-
tion of the franchise, which, indeed, has never had
a more unfaltering opponent. From first to last
he opposed parliamentary reform in any shape,
and even declared that he would prefer ' to add to
the weight and independency of the voters by
lessening their numbers.'[3]   He could sound a warning note, when pleading for relief of the Irish
Catholics, that ' half-citizens ' may be made ' whole

[1] *Regicide Peace*, Letter i.   [2] *Ibid.*, Letter iii.
[3] He at any rate says that such is the view of ' most sober
thinkers.'—*Observations*.

Jacobins ' ; [1] but a similar fear seems never to have disturbed his mind in regard to the masses of his unenfranchised countrymen whether Catholics or Protestants.

We have here, in fact, in undiluted form, the Whig theory of political trusteeship. A British public of 400,000 souls ; within that a select electorate ; within that, again, a still more select body of representatives of constituencies ; and the peers to complete the representation (for he sometimes at any rate [2] claimed that they were truly representative of the people) with the king as keystone of the arch—these were the hands into which the trust of the nation's destinies was, and ought to be, confided. Whatsoever is more than this cometh of evil.

Nor does the matter rest here. For there is a further aristocratic note in the demand that the representative, however select his constituency, must never be degraded into the delegate. There is nothing in all his writings on which Burke more vehemently insists than this. By all means let electorates express their grievances, wants, and demands, both on their own account and on that of the larger British public behind them ; by all means let them watch how their representatives vote,[3]

[1] Letter to William Smith.

[2] *Thoughts on the Present Discontents* : ' The King is the representative of the people ; so are the lords ; so are the judges. They are all trustees for the people.'

[3] *Thoughts.* It was at this time he urged the importance of frequent and correct lists of the votes given in all important divisions.

but let them never presume to dictate to the men of
their choice how these things are to be dealt with
and remedied. It was his boast that he was the
first man who, on the hustings, rejected the authority of instructions from constituents.[1] And he
proved the sincerity of his words by the sacrifice of
his seat at Bristol. ' Depend upon it the lovers of
freedom will be free '—this is what he told his
constituents. And the freedom he claimed was
nothing less than the liberty to serve them by the
exercise of his own judgment—a judgment un-
pledged and unmortgaged not only, be it noted, on
points of detail, but on matters of general policy.
He stoutly refused to admit that he ever *followed*
the sense of his constituency ; he prefers to say that
his opinions ' met theirs upon the way.' [2] ' No
man,' he once declared, ' carries further than I do
the policy of making government pleasing to the
people. But the widest range of this politic com-
plaisance is confined within the limits of justice.
I would not only consult the interest of the people,
but I would cheerfully gratify their humours. We
are all a sort of children that must be soothed and
managed. I think I am not austere or formal in
my nature. I would bear, I would even myself

[1] *Appeal.*

[2] Speech on the Economical Reform. Cf. Speech, Feb. 6,
1772. ' The ground for a legislative alteration of a legal establishment is this and this only : that you find the inclinations
of the majority of the people, concurring with your own sense of
the intolerable nature of the abuse, are in favour of a change.'

play my part in, any innocent buffoonery to divert them. But I never will act the tyrant for their amusement. If they will mix malice in their sports, I shall never consent to throw them any living sentient creature whatsoever, no, not so much as a kitling, to torment.' [1]

Hence not only a hatred of pledges such as would shock a modern caucus, but an unbending antagonism to shortening of parliaments, and to every other democratic device whereby the lovers of freedom could be transformed into the slaves of constituencies. ' To minimise confidence—to maximise control '—this was afterwards the panacea of Bentham. Burke would reverse the formula. *His* policy was to maximise confidence—to minimise control. The good citizen after Bentham's heart was to deem it a civic duty ' to make public functionaries uneasy ' : this is *his* version of responsibility to the people. One wonders if he had read Burke's trenchant judgment, that to dream of securing genuine and honourable service by that kind of responsibility is worthy of ' none but idiots.' [2]

It is important, however, to bear in mind upon what this plea for the independence of the representative rests. Not, as it sometimes does, on the notion that an elector is not necessarily a statesman, which indeed is obvious, but on the deeper ground that it is essential to all statesmanship to act on

---

[1] Speech at Bristol, 1780.　　　　[2] *Reflections.*

principles, and on the final resort upon ' the eternal
rules of justice and reason,' which he has told us
are above not only the will of electorates, but above
all orders in the State.[1] For it is not only because
he has to deal with problems far beyond the powers
of the average elector that the representative must
be free. He must also enjoy the far higher freedom
of setting his feet, independently, on principles which
have a deeper source than popular verdicts. Nothing can be more explicit than his statements here.
' The votes of a majority of the people, whatever
their infamous flatterers may teach in order to
corrupt their minds, cannot alter the moral any
more than they can alter the physical essence of
things.' [2] A second sentence is even more specific.
' Neither the few nor the many have a right to act
merely by their will in any matter connected with
duty, trust, engagement, or obligation.' [3] For the
final appeal in politics lies, not with the voice of
electorates, but with the lessons of history, and the
eternal laws of reason and justice, of which all
human laws are but declaratory.[4] It is essential to
remember this, because otherwise some of Burke's
more democratic sentences would be misleading. ' I
reverentially look up to the opinion of the people,'
he once declared, ' and with an awe that is almost

[1] P. 162.   [2] *Appeal.*   [3] *Ibid.*
[4] *Tracts on the Popery Laws.* All human laws are, properly
speaking, only declaratory : they may alter the mode and application, but have no power over the substance of original justice.'

superstitious.' [1] So he did, if by ' opinion of the
people ' be meant their feelings, their wishes, their
sense of grievance or their sense of justice. Did he
not say that he did not know the way to draw up
an indictment against a whole people ? Did he not
say that in all disputes between the people and their
rulers ' the presumption is at least upon a par in
favour of the people'; and add that ' where popular
discontents have been very prevalent . . . there
has been generally something found amiss in the
constitution, or in the conduct of government ' ? [2]
Yet, when ' opinion ' be taken to mean a definite
judgment on a matter either of principle or policy,
it is not reverence that describes his attitude : it
is something that savours of contempt : ' We are
not to go to school to them to learn the principles
of law and government. . . . As to the detail of
particular measures, or to any general schemes of
policy, they have neither enough of speculation in the
closet, nor of experience in business, to decide upon
it. They can well see whether we are tools of a
court or their honest servants. Of that they can
well judge, and I wish that they always exercised
their judgment ; but of the particular merits of a
measure, I have other standards.' [3] Hardly could
there be a more explicit repudiation of the notion
that a parliament of freemen can ever be made
out of an assembly of delegates.

[1] Speech on the Duration of Parliaments.
[2] *Present Discontents.* [3] *Ibid.*

If this be Burke's attitude to the electorate, we can easily understand why he should view the existence of an immense non-electorate with equanimity. Sometimes he will have it that it is just as good for these subjects who are not citizens, nay, better, to be *virtually* represented by the men chosen by a limited electorate in which they have no part.[1] Sometimes he would persuade them that nothing is more certain than that their lives would be no happier with votes than without them. And sometimes he frankly, though with the utmost goodwill, pronounces them altogether incapable of exercising political functions. ' How can he get wisdom that holdeth the plough and that glorieth in the goad ; that driveth oxen and is occupied in their labours ; and whose talk is of bullocks ? '—he quotes the words,[2] and there is no mistaking the sincerity of his approval of them.

And yet it was from no lack of sympathy with men, even though their talk was of bullocks, that Burke would thus shut the door of citizenship in the face of the great mass of his fellow-countrymen. He was one of the most human-hearted of all our

[1] Virtual representation plays so large a part in the Whig scheme of things that it is interesting to have Burke's definition : ' Virtual representation is that in which there is a communion of interest, and a sympathy in feelings and desires between those who act in the name of any description of people, and the people in whose name they act, though the trustees are not actually chosen by them.'—Letter to Langrishe.

[2] *Reflections.*

great men. None has ever more consistently lived
up to his own demand, that the statesman ought
to love and respect his kind. Once, in a speech,[1]
he had occasion to refer to the wish of Henry IV.
of France that he might live to see a fowl in the
pot of every peasant in his kingdom. 'That sentiment of homely benevolence,' so runs his comment,
'was worth all the splendid sayings that are recorded of kings.' Few men of any kind, be their
radicalism never so keen, have had in equal measure
the gift of being personally at home with all sorts
and conditions of men. And he carried these
feelings into his politics. Though he could not
value the votes of humble men, he never could
forget their interests. 'When the smallest rights
of the poorest people in the kingdom are in question, I would set my face against any act of pride
and power countenanced by the highest that are
in it ; and, if it should come to the last extremity
and to a contest of blood, God forbid ! God forbid !
—my part is taken ; I would take my part with
the poor and low and feeble.'[2] This was not the
voice of rhetoric. It was the expression of a profound sympathy with humble life, which began in
early years in his Irish home, and lasted till the
end. All his experience of life convinced him that
human happiness and worth were by no means

[1] On Fox's East India Bill.
[2] Speech on the Marriage Act, 1781.

oftenest found along the paths that lead either to
riches or distinction or power. We have already
met the declaration that 'the true moral equality
of man' lay in the happiness that was to be found
by virtue in all conditions ; and in the same strain
is his retort upon certain persons who, with a
patronising and 'puling jargon' (or what he regarded as such), had been talking of 'the labour-
ing poor.' 'I do not call a healthy young man,
cheerful in his mind and vigorous in his arms, I
cannot call such a man poor : I cannot pity my
kind as a kind merely because they are men.' [1]

But moral sympathy with men is one thing, and
the political sympathy that takes the form of
giving them votes is another ; and, in Burke, the
two lie far asunder. As in some other Conservatives
of genius, Scott or Johnson or Wordsworth (in his
later years), the love of men goes hand in hand
with a hatred of wide franchises. His disbelief in
count of heads is as inveterate as Carlyle's. Neither
in right nor in reason is the verdict of numbers
justifiable. Not in *right*, because as the natural
right of every man to a vote is a sheer fiction, the
units can never claim, *on grounds of right*, that they
are each and all to be counted as participants in
any decision whatsoever. And not in *reason*,
because, when the principle that the majority
ought to prevail is adopted (as of course is often

[1] *Regicide Peace*, Letter III.

enough the case), this, as matter of fact, implies a civil society already constituted. And a civil society is so far from being constituted on the arithmetical plan that it is of its essence to reflect inevitable distinctions between man and man, or class and class, such as render it, absurd to ignore their inequalities. And amongst these differences none are, in Burke's eyes, more pronounced than the having, or the lacking, capacity for the exercise of political power. We have seen already how convinced he was that the qualities that fit a man for even the passive citizenship that does no more than go to the poll, were far from widely diffused, and how decisively he consigned the multitude to the two large categories, ' the objects of protection,' and ' the means of force.'

The other side of this distrust of the multitude is his pronounced faith in the leadership of the few. For leadership is, in the very nature of things, a comparatively rare thing even amongst those who are within the pale of the constitution. It is in fact the natural monopoly of that limited number who enjoy opportunities for the experience of affairs, and for that face-to-face contact with those practical problems of public moment which are the seed-plot of that ' prudence ' which is the supreme virtue of the statesman. And if this path be closed, as closed it is, in Burke's estimate of human nature, to the vast majority of the British public, to them

the needful political wisdom will never come. It
will not come even when there are opportunities of
birth, leisure, wealth, or natural gifts, if these opportunities be not utilised. Burke was far enough
from thinking all noblemen Solons, or all nabobs
statesmen. But he never doubted that, from those
classes where such opportunities were forthcoming,
there would always emerge a supply of ' men of light
and leading ' (the phrase is his), in whose hands the
government of the nation could be confidently reposed. For it is an article of his political faith that,
by the constitution of human nature, and by the
laws of social struggle and growth, every society
may be counted upon to produce a ' natural aristocracy.' Inevitably the inborn and ineffaceable inequalities of men assert themselves ; inevitably
opportunity evokes practical ability ; inevitably
the ' discipline of Nature,' working throughout the
generations of a nation's life, sifts out the classes and
the men who are fit to lead and govern from the
rest whose lot it is to follow and be governed. The
result is the emergence of that ' natural aristocracy,' of which the aristocracy of birth and wealth
is only a part. And fortunately, Burke has set
down his conception of what this larger aristocracy
can be in words of which it is not too much to say
that they exalt our idea of human nature. ' A true,
natural aristocracy is not a separate interest in the
State, or separable from it. It is an essential in-

tegrant part of any large body rightly constituted. It is formed out of a class of legitimate presumptions, presumptions, which, taken as generalities, must be admitted for actual truths. To be bred in a place of estimation ; to see nothing low and sordid from one's infancy ; to be taught to respect one's self ; to be habituated to the censorial inspection of the public eye ; to look early to public opinion ; to stand upon such elevated ground as to be enabled to take a large view of the widespread and infinitely diversified combinations of men and affairs in a large society ; to have leisure to read, to reflect, to converse ; to be enabled to draw the court and attention of the wise and learned wherever they are to be found ;—to be habituated in armies, to command and to obey ; to be taught to despise danger in the pursuit of honour and duty ; to be formed to the greatest degree of vigilance, foresight, and circumspection, in a state of things in which no fault is committed with impunity, and the slightest mistakes draw on the most ruinous conse- quences ;—to be led to a guarded and regulated con- duct, from a sense that you are considered as an instructor of your fellow-citizens in their highest concerns, and that you act as a reconciler between God and man ;—to be employed as an administrator of law and justice, and to be thereby amongst the first benefactors to mankind ;—to be a professor of high science, or of liberal and ingenuous art ;—to be amongst rich traders, who from their success are presumed to have sharp and vigorous understandings, and to possess the virtues of diligence, order, constancy, and regularity, and to have cultivated an habitual regard to commutative justice :—these are the circumstances of men that form what I should call a *natural* aristocracy, without which there is no nation.' [1]

It was to the light and leading of this class, supported by a limited electorate, and a larger, though still limited, ' British public,' that Burke was well content to entrust the happiness and government of the British people.   It was the same position as he had taken up in one of his earliest writings [2] when he declared ' the natural strength of the kingdom ' to lie in ' the great peers, the leading landed gentlemen, the opulent merchants and manufacturers, the substantial yeomanry.'

For government thus constituted, Burke has a profound respect.   It is a great art : it is ' an agency of beneficence,' it is ' a contrivance of human wisdom to provide for human wants.'   But these and many other similar words must not convey the impression that he was by any means of the number of those who think that even the best of governments can do everything.   On the contrary he sometimes

[1] *Appeal.*
[2] *Thoughts on the Cause of the Present Discontents.*

estimates the functions of government surprisingly low. ' To provide for us in our necessities,' he writes in the *Thoughts on Scarcity*, ' is not in the power of government. It would be a vain presumption in statesmen to think they can do it. The people maintain them, and not they the people. It is in the power of government to prevent much evil; it can do very little positive good in this, or perhaps in anything else.' ' Laws,' he says elsewhere, ' cannot make men rich or happy, that they must do for themselves.' [1] There are pages, indeed, in which he is almost Cobdenite in his jealousy of interference with trade : ' My opinion is against an overdoing of any sort of administration, and more especially against this most momentous of all meddling on the part of authority, the meddling with the subsistence of the people.' [2] And, in the same spirit, ' wise and salutary neglect' would be his policy in governing the colonies. Nor is it the least of his indictments of the radical reformers that they recklessly excite vain expectations which political reform is impotent to fulfil. He was, indeed, always convinced that the happiness of a people has its springs in many sources which lie quite beyond the competence of either legislation or administration. Though ' a society without government,' that aspiration of Godwinian circles was in his eyes no better than the vagary of a metaphysical

---

[1] Letter to Nagle.   [2] *Thoughts on Scarcity.*

madman ; he was far from the thought that government and society are co-extensive.

In one respect, indeed, he would limit the province of government quite narrowly. Seldom, almost never, ought a government to take upon itself the task of any large reconstruction of the constitution. For reasons we have seen.[1] In the first place it could not do it, were it to try. For that most complex and delicately balanced mechanism or organism, the constitution of a civil society, is so great a miracle of gradual experimental contrivance and workmanship, that it defies the utmost skill of any man or group of men, to refashion it *de novo*. And, in the second place, it ought not to try, because it is of the essence of political wisdom to regard the constitution as it stands, as the product, not only of human wisdom working through the centuries, but of that Higher Power which presides over all human affairs, and, by its guidance, not only justifies, but consecrates the achievements of historic peoples. It follows that it is the paramount duty of men in power to accept the constitution as it stands as an ' entailed inheritance,' and to transmit it, substantially unaltered, to their successors.

Hence it would seem that there is nothing left for governments to do but to administer this constitution as a trust, and to bring its administration to the highest pitch of justice and efficiency. Nor can

[1] P. 68 *et seq.*.

there be a doubt that this is, in effect, the net
result of Burke's teaching. The line he draws
between constitutional and administrative reform
is deep and final ; and whatever may be done in
the province of administration, the constitution of
his eulogies, again and again reiterated, must stand
unchanged in all essentials. Strange doctrine this
for latter-day radicals, and even for nineteenth-
century Whigs, who have seen the constitution
again and again reformed within a century, and
seem even yet to be far from satisfied that they have
touched the forever-flying limits of finality.

There are, however, some considerations which
greatly modify this otherwise unbending, not to
say impossible, conservatism. In the first place,
it does not follow that government need find its
occupation gone. A truism perhaps—yet a truism
that needs resuscitation. For, since the middle of
the nineteenth century, the activity of legislatures
has become so conspicuous a fact that the citizens
of all progressive states run some risk of falling
victims to the fallacy that, if a government does not
produce legislative novelties, it exists for no purpose :
so much so, that parliamentary criticism and control
of ministers, in their administrative capacity, is not
seldom resented as if it were flagitious waste of
time subtracted from the carrying through of organic
reforms. The needful reminder is that, without
prejudice to organic legislation (which doubtless

has its claims), governments exist to administer, and that no time, trouble, or industry can be too great to ensure that their administration be just, efficient, and pure. For constitutions are not reformed only by reform of the constitution. Constitutions are made to march. Nor is this trite reflection ever in more need of resurrection than in days when party is tempted to bid against party, and partisan against partisan, in the competitive auction-room of constitutional agitation and reform.

This was a point that Burke realised. It was not because he hated reform that he resisted reform of the constitution. Partly, at any rate, it was because as a man of affairs he saw how much might be done by reform of administration. He proved this by his deeds. For when his party at last came into power, he grappled with administrative reform with a tenacity and thoroughness which can never be forgotten, because happily they stand recorded in that speech on Economic Reform, which is a monument of reforming statesmanship. And this was but one enterprise among many. Buckle's catalogue of his reforms, already quoted,[1] is proof enough not only that he found reforming work to do, but that the spirit of reform was in him, and that it burned with so strong a flame that the wonder grows that he could restrain it so effectually within limits, and stop short, with an all but absolute *non*

[1] P. 77.

possumus, the moment reform would touch the constitution. This, however, is precisely what he did. Not because of the spectre of the French Revolution, as is sometimes supposed, but from convictions formed long before it was so much as above the horizon, he stood throughout his life, firm, not to say fierce, in his antipathy to constitutional reform. To organise and to purify administration ; to exercise administrative powers ; to safeguard civil rights ; to ensure toleration (except for infidels and atheists) ; to be ready to wage war, and to wage it with courage and pertinacity ; to tax with wisdom and equity ; to free trade from restrictions ; to redress grievances and correct abuses ; to call public servants to account ; and, not least, to jealously prevent any element in the body-politic —king, lords, commons, populace, landed interests, or landless interest or any other interest—from usurping more than its appropriate place and function—these things, and such as these, are within the scope of government. But to remake the constitution, or even to touch it with radical hands— this is folly, fanaticism, and sacrilege.

Whatever be the justification of this attitude in theory, or relatively to the circumstances of the age, it was not, as every schoolboy knows, found tenable in practice. Even whilst Burke was reiterating in many a glowing page his liturgy to the English constitution in all its unreformed perfection of Whig franchise, rotten burghs, and corrupt representatives, forces which have proved irresistible were beginning to shift the centre of political gravity. The expansion of industry and commerce, sometimes called the industrial revolution, was rapidly multiplying and bringing to the front a new aristocracy of wealth and middle-class comfort, with whom the landed aristocracy and their dependents were constrained in 1832 to share their supremacy. History was deaf to Burke's appeal to the old Whigs. And, after no long interval, the new oligarchy of lords, squires, capitalists, and well-to-do shop-keepers was in its turn persuaded, without much resistance, to take into partnership, first the artisans in 1867, and then the agricultural labourers in 1884. The 'glorious constitution,' which Bentham declared 'needed to be looked into,' was 'looked into' to some purpose, and the constitution of Burke's idolatry transformed to its foundations. Much of this the reforming Whigs of the nineteenth century themselves recognised as reasonable as well as inevitable. Macaulay is typical. For though Macaulay is as zealous to preserve the continuity of the constitution as Burke, he had come to think (with Lord Holland) that 'large exclusions would destroy the constitution if it did not destroy them.' Hence in his oration in support of the Reform Bill of 1832, his impassioned appeal to the Tories takes the form of telling them that if they would conserve the constitution they must reform it. Nay, he was quite prepared to surrender the Whig illusion of 'finality,' and to declare for the reopening of the settlement of 1832. 'We shall make our institutions more democratic than they are,' he wrote in 1852, 'not by lowering the franchise to the level of the great mass of the community, but by raising, in a time which will be very short when compared with the history of a nation, the great mass up to the level of the franchise.' The words point the contrast between the reforming Whig of the nineteenth, and the conservative Whig of the eighteenth century. For though Burke was in many directions as zealous a reformer, and a far greater force in politics than Macaulay, he had nothing but an iron welcome for reformers of the constitution. To conserve the constitution by reforming it, and to reform it by raising the great mass up to the level of the franchise, were things that were only dreamt of in his philosophy as a monstrous usurpation. 'Well to know the best time and manner of yielding what it is impossible to keep '—this was his own criterion of a wise government.[1] But, then, he never had a doubt that it was as possible as it was desirable to keep the constitution of the eighteenth century.

The difficulty of justifying Burke's position here is of his own making; for it does not arise from

[1] *Economical Reform,*

his desire to perpetuate the old Whig constitution, which might be allowed to have its merits, but from his determination to do this, and, at the same time, to find a place, and that a large place, for reform. For though it is obvious enough that much may be done for a country by reforms which do not seriously, or at all directly, touch its political constitution, nothing is more certain than that such reforms, if they be reforms, must alter the actual strength of social and political forces. And once these forces are altered, it is only a matter of time that the change should reflect itself on the political constitution. Reforms that make for the freeing of trade, or for the recognition of combinations of workmen, are not constitutional reforms. They might be carried through by constitutional conservation. But if the results be the growth of an influential class of rich traders, or the rise of organisations of labour, it is not in the nature of things that the members of either of these classes should for long sit down content under a political system which denies them adequate political power and representation. Sooner or later the cry, so dear to Bentham, of ' No Monopoly ' is raised. The ' monopoly ' might vary. In the sixteenth century it had been the monopoly of Catholic against Protestant, and in the seventeenth the royal monopoly of Divine right. In the nineteenth it was to be the monopoly of Protestant against Catholic, of Tory and Whig borough-mongers against non-electors, of landed food-producers against food-consumers, of capitalists against labour. And once that cry is caught up and re-echoed by large classes who have come to a consciousness of their social value and influence, the hour has come when, in Macaulay's words, the political constitution must destroy exclusions, or exclusions will destroy it. With this spirit Burke went a certain length. He hated any revival of royal prerogative ; he hated a domineering House of Commons ; he hated religious intolerance ; he hated the penal code that crushed the Irish Catholics ; he hated negro slavery ; he hated the restrictions that strangled commerce. Nay, he has himself left words which are obviously the source of Lord Holland's remark : ' Our constitution is not made for great general or proscriptive exclusions ; sooner or later it will destroy them, or they will destroy the constitution.' [1] When he wrote these words, his thoughts, we must suppose, did not travel beyond the question that evoked them —the admission of the Irish Catholics to the franchise. But their wisdom is so unimpeachable, and their wider applications so natural, that they come with something of a surprise from the greatest of all the apologists of Whig monopoly.

And yet there need be no surprise, not at any rate for the reader who recalls the many passages

[1] Letter to Sir H. Langrishe.

in which Burke expresses the conviction that, in all civil societies worthy of the name, the individual must expect to find himself committed to many ties and obligations not of his own making, and yet not to be repudiated without a breach of the fundamental duties of life. 'Look through the whole of life,' he says, 'and the whole system of duties. Much the strongest moral obligations are such as were never the results of our option.'[1] And these duties were not limited to the private relationships of life, those, for example, of parents to children and children to parents, which he cites in illustration; they extend to the public duties as well. 'If,' so runs the context, 'the social ties and ligaments, spun out of those physical relations which are the elements of the commonwealth, in most cases begin, and always continue, independently of our will, so, without any stipulation on our own part, are we bound by that relation, called our country, which comprehends (as it has been well said) all the charities of all.'[2] Nor does he cease to press the point till his sentences read almost, if not altogether, as if they were a plea for finding the whole duty of man in an acceptance by the individual of his divinely allotted station in a social system, which it was not for him to alter or even criticise. Two results follow : *the first*, that duty and will, duty and option, duty and choice, are thrown into

[1] *Appeal.*   [2] *Ibid.*

such antithesis that duty and will are said to be
'even contradictory terms'; [1] *the second*, that
government by consent, if it is to be accepted, as
it was accepted, by all good Whigs, must not be
held to imply—as radicals might suggest—that the
members of a society are not really free until the
laws and the constitution under which they have
to live, have become a matter of will, choice, or
option. Such choice, such option is, in Burke's
eyes at any rate, neither practicable nor desirable.

Nor can it be denied that, within limits, this line
of argument is forcible. Government by consent,
if consent means individual choice, option, or explicit
contract, is an impossible thing. Even in the most
democratic state the citizen must expect to find himself accepting much to which he is not, in this sense,
consenting. He may be one of a minority that
accepts measures passed by a majority from which
he vehemently dissents. He may be represented
by a man whom he detests, and has done his best to
defeat at the poll. He may be wholly out of sympathy with some of the leaders of his own party,
from which he is nevertheless by no means ready
to revolt. He may even—who can deny it ?—be
sorrowfully convinced that reforms of great abuses
are still, by the force of circumstances, quite beyond
the horizon of practical politics. He may still, of
course, believe that the government under which he

[1] P. 91.

lives is government by consent, but it is, all too clearly, likewise government bound up with much to which he is not consenting. Similarly, though in greatly magnified degree, with Burke. He saw that government by consent must needs involve for individuals many obligations to which they are not consenting. Only, having made this point good, he went on to include within its scope the whole system of Whig trusteeship, with its limited franchise and prescriptive aristocratic ascendency. It may be that, in insisting upon this, he makes his position untenable. To this we shall return. But this is no reason for supposing him to have ever parted company with his orthodox Whig faith in government by consent. The correct inference is that he was convinced that government by consent was, beyond all doubt, more substantially realised under Whig trusteeship, with its 'virtual representation,' than under any substitute which innovating radicalism, with its untried democratic franchises, was likely to put in its place.

It has been said by some that the Whigs had no foundations : Johnson said so when he called his friend a 'bottomless Whig.' It has been also said that they did not even miss the absence of foundations : Carlyle said as much when he dubbed them 'amateurs' and 'dilettanti'; and James Mill said something more when he indulged all the pleasures of malevolence in fastening upon the whole hateful connection the imputation of 'trimming,' 'see-sawing,' 'jesuitry of politics,' and much else to the same effect. But whatever truth may underlie the impeachment, the Whigs are not without their rejoinder. It is always open to them to point to the fact that if ever any statesman had foundations it was Burke, and that Burke's theory of government, be its value what it may, had its foundations deeply laid in his conception of a people, and in the profoundly conservative principles deducible therefrom.

CHAPTER X

RIGHTS

(a) *What are the Rights of Man?*

GOVERNMENT and rights are, needless to say, things closely related ; and the relation is at its closest and simplest in Bentham.   For to that great law reformer, as is well known, all rights were derivative. They were the creatures of legislation, and as such could not so much as exist prior to a legislating government.   ' Real laws give birth to real rights.' [1] And from this it followed that all other ' rights ' not thus derived, and in particular the ' rights of man ' of the radicals of the Revolution, were no better than the flimsiest of fictions.   For, if these rights of man are dignified as antecedent to all law and all government, they would be prior to their own creator.   It was thus that this great radical showed himself so eager to convert the world to the radicalism of utility, that he did not hesitate to overturn the radicalism of ' natural rights ' to its foundations.

Now, if we compare this doctrine with that which

[1] *Theory of Legislation,* p. 85.

may be gathered from many pages of Burke, nothing is easier than to develop a contrast. Nowhere do we find Burke committing himself to a doctrine so extreme as that there are no real rights but legal rights ; and nowhere do we find him asseverating that the natural rights of man do not so much as exist except as the ' anarchical fallacies ' of fools and fanatics. On the contrary, he not only asserts, but reiterates in explicit terms, that man does possess rights, even before civil society comes into being. Not only does he say that rights are ' natural ' and that natural rights are ' sacred ' [1]— an admission that perhaps counts for little so long as the ambiguous word ' natural ' is undefined—he does not dispute the doctrine, that very doctrine so dear to the hearts of Rousseau and Paine and all their following, that men have ' primitive ' rights, and that, in becoming members of a civil society, they may be regarded as surrendering certain of these rights in order to secure the right of citizens who live under the protection of the laws of the State. His words admit of no other interpretation : ' One of the first motives to civil society, and which becomes one of its fundamental rules, is that no man should be judge in his own cause. By this each person has at once divested himself of the first fundamental right of uncovenanted man, that is, to judge for himself, and to assert his own cause. He

[1] Speech on Mr. Fox's East India Bill.

abdicates all right to be his own governor. He inclusively, in a great measure, abandons the right to self-defence, the first law of nature. Men cannot enjoy the rights of an uncivil and of a civil state together. That he may obtain justice, he gives up his right of determining what it is, in points the most essential to him. That he may secure some liberty, he makes a surrender in trust of the whole of it. Government is not made in virtue of natural rights, which may, and do exist in total independence of it ; and exist in much greater clearness, and in a much greater degree of abstract perfection : but their abstract perfection is their practical defeat.' [1] ' Liberty,' he says in another passage, ' must be limited in order to be possessed.' [2]

From sentences like these (and there are others to the same effect) it is evident that conservative Burke is by no means so flatly hostile to the doctrine of the natural rights of man as radical Bentham. He does not, like that ' great subversive,' shake the very dust of the doctrine off his feet.

And yet, as all the world knows, Burke's antipathy to this doctrine is extreme. In the bitterness of his detestation of it he out - Benthams Bentham ; nor can all the records of political controversy furnish stronger language than that which he hurls at its apostles. Almost he would persuade us that they and it are Antichrist. This being so,

[1] *Reflections.*   [2] Letter to the Sheriffs.

the question that emerges is obvious. If he admits, as we have just seen he does admit, that men possess ' primitive rights,' ' rights of uncovenanted man,' rights that belong to persons ' in total independence of government,' rights that have to be surrendered in passing into civil society, why this bitterness, this implacable hostility, this denunciation ? Manifestly he does not hold, as Bentham did, that these rights have no existence. Why, then, should he cry havoc on the men who made it their business to declare them to the world ?

In answering this question it is essential, to begin with, to bear in mind that Burke does not attack the doctrine as a theorist denouncing a theory, but as a politician whose interest is fixed on the application of the doctrine to politics. Had the theory of natural rights been merely academic, as many theories are, we should have heard little about it from him. For abstract theorising he declared that he had neither inclination—which was partially true ; nor competence—which was manifestly false. Therefore, it was not for him to enter upon abstract arguments, and far less to construct an abstract theory of natural rights. Not without an edge of irony, he left all that ' to the Schools,' and to the high and reverend authorities who lift up their heads on one side or the other, only to end by floundering in ' the great Serbonian Bog, where armies whole have sunk.' This was his consistent attitude. But, then, *this* theory was not like other theories. It was a theory that had been adopted as a political gospel. It was the inspiration of a proselytising movement, and the watchword, not to say the ultimatum of a party in the State. Far from being meant for the consumpt only of professors, theorists, and students, it was the core of the political evangel of Rousseau, the inspiration of the incendiary *Rights of Man* of Paine, and the text of sermons preached to ' the gentlemen of the Society for Revolutions.' It had descended, and it was meant by its votaries to descend, from the study to the market-place, and had become the daily bread of radical reformers who seemed bent upon transforming society to its foundations, not in France alone or England, but over the length and breadth of Europe ; and the inferences of its zealots lay in their passions. It has often enough been said that the theory of the rights of man is the most convincing proof that theory, so far from being impotent, as fools and Philistines aver, is capable of revolutionising the world. This was what Burke saw ; this was what he feared.[1] He was not, in his assault upon the rights of man, criticising a theory ; he was resisting a political propaganda which seemed to him to be fraught with

[1] See *Thoughts on French Affairs* : ' It is a revolution of doctrine and theoretic dogma. It has a much greater resemblance to those changes which have been made upon religious grounds, in which a spirit of proselytism makes an essential part.'

catastrophe for Europe. His dominant interest is always practical. Clearly we must, therefore, not expect a theoretical discussion of rights from him.

Nevertheless he is forced, almost in his own despite, if not to cross the line that parts practice from theory, at any rate to press into the interesting borderland where these two meet. For when a controversialist has to encounter a theory that is also a political programme, he cannot separate the programme from the theory. He finds himself in the presence of urgent demands which claim to be rights, and of which the validity has to be discussed. It is so here. Burke found himself in the presence of many claims which the revolutionists declared to be rights, and which he believed not to be rights at all. And in resisting these with all the forces of his reasoning and rhetoric he takes up a line of argument which is in no slight measure theoretical.

This line of argument is quite firm and definite. Refusing, as he always refused, to be drawn into an academic discussion of the abstract rights of man pure and simple—he ' hates the very sound of them,'—he plants himself on the conception of man as essentially a member of a civil society. ' I have in my contemplation,' he declares, ' the civil social man and no other.' [1] In other words, the only rights, or claims to rights, he was prepared, or even had the patience, to discuss, were those rights

[1] *Reflections.*

which were either actually enjoyed, or could be
enjoyed, or ought to be enjoyed by the members
of an actual organised society. That there were
'natural' rights, 'original' rights, 'rights of uncovenanted man,' 'rights held in total independence of government,' he did not deny. He affirms,
as we have just seen, that such rights exist. He
even specifies what some of them are (the right of
self-defence, for example). But the right of self-
defence, as it appears in its empty generality in
the abstract and hypothetical code of a theorist is
one thing, and the same right, as it appears articu-
lated, defined, modified, abated in the eyes of a
man of affairs who is working for the concrete
happiness of an actual people under given conditions
of place and time—this is quite another thing. And
it is this second thing, this definition of rights with
reference to the actual social situation, that is always
in Burke's eyes by far the most important matter,
and, indeed, the only question of real political
moment. To keep ever before his eyes 'the civil
social man and no other,' and in the light of this
to discriminate between the claims that are to be
justified and upheld and the claims that are to be
resisted and discredited—this is of the essence of
Burke's entire treatment of rights.

It is this that explains his decisive divergence
from the apostles of the rights of man. His attitude
is not Bentham's. He does not meet their asser-

tion that all men have natural rights by the blunt
counter-assertion that no man has any. His quarrel
with them turns not on their general assertion that
men have natural rights, but on the impeachment that
first they went to work to dogmatise a whole abstract
a priori code of rights, and then, having formulated
this to their own satisfaction, went on to announce it
to the world as a political ultimatum which it was
the duty of every reformer and the central function
of all law and government to enact *quam primum*.
On both points he joins issue. He believes that for
any practical or statesmanlike purpose it is a barren
enterprise (even though it may interest some
' metaphysical ' minds) to theorise a code of rights
in abstracto and without reference not only to
social conditions in general, but to the specific
conditions of some actual society. And he equally
insists—indeed it is only the same point in another
aspect—that a given civil society is so far from
being an agency for realising a code of rights already
framed and formulated in abstraction, that it is
only in and through his participation in the life
of an actual society that an individual, be his
abstract hypothetical rights what they may, can
acquire any rights that are definite, substantial,
and worth the possessing. Hence the antithesis
that the ' abstract perfection ' of a right, such as
the right of self-defence, is its practical defeat. It
is only a forcible way of saying that the more per-

fectly any right, by process of abstraction, escapes from the limitations of concrete circumstances, the more are the limitations which it must encounter in finding realisation in any given actual social system. Similarly with the kindred assertion that every man ' surrenders ' or ' abdicates ' the rights of uncovenanted man in becoming a member of a civil society. For this, too, is but another way of saying that an absolutely unrestricted liberty of self-assertion is manifestly incompatible with the fact that any such impracticable liberty must be ' limited in order to be enjoyed ' by the members of a civil society who must needs stand in limiting relations one to another.

Nor is this ' surrender ' or ' abdication ' to be deplored as if it were a calamity. For the liberty that is surrendered is after all an empty, just because it is a purely abstract liberty, and the liberty for which this is exchanged is the liberty of enjoying all the liberties and rights of an actual civil society. And it is these, these rights of the civil social man and none other, that are the real concern of statesmen, legislators, judges, and citizens.

For when the question, What are the legitimate rights of men ? is raised, not by abstract theorists, whose interest is speculative, but, as in Burke's day, by practical politicians who are dealing with the happiness of an actual civil society, there are two widely divergent directions in which an answer may be sought. If we take the one, we go to the dicta of dogmatists, or to the codes, declarations, or preambles of constitutions which these dogmatists inspire, and which simply set down the rights of man as if they were a revelation that stood in need of no further examination and proof, and as if every descendant of Adam were defrauded of his birthright, so long as one single right thus dogmatised is denied or withheld. If we take the other, we follow the lead of the more cautious and reflective minds, whose prime concern is the civil social man and none other, and with whom it is a settled principle to refuse to accept any claim whatever as a right, until by a scrutiny of human nature and the social system with which they have to deal, they have satisfied themselves on the one hand that their fellowmen have the capacity to enjoy it, and on the other that the enjoyment of it is consistent with the conditions and the ends of the given society in which their lot is cast.

Needless to say that it is in the second of these directions we must turn if we follow the lead of Burke. For from the many pages of his invective against the radicalism of the rights of man there emerge two articles of indictment which, if true, convict his adversaries of two inexcusable and blundering omissions. The one is that, in thinking so much about man's abstract rights, they did not think enough about his nature. 'That sort of people,' he says, 'are so taken up with their theories about the rights of man that they have totally forgot his nature.'[1] In other words, they dogmatised about rights when they had been better occupied in studying the fitness of actual men to enjoy and use them. The second impeachment is that, in their fanatical impatience to force their cut-and-dried code of rights, their 'little catechism of the rights of man,' upon the world, they could not, or would not, stop to inquire if the realisation of their programme was consistent with the fundamental facts and conditions of the existing social order. 'How,' he asks, 'can any man claim, under the conventions of civil society, rights which do not so much as presuppose its existence. Rights which are absolutely repugnant to it ? '[2] On both these points, as indeed must be already evident, his own position is irreconcilably antagonistic. He thought he knew something about human nature, and one of the facts which he saw written on its very forefront was endless inequality of powers, capacities, and achievement, and, not least conspicuous, inequality in political capacity. This alone was enough to demolish, in his eyes, the 'monstrous fiction' of equality of *political* rights. It was against all reason to assert that all men have a right to the franchise, if, by virtue of the imperfections that cleave to their human nature, ignorance, for

[1] *Reflections.* [2] *Ibid.*

example, or indifference or absorption in toil, they
were inherently incapable of exercising it. So far
was it from being inconsistent, in his eyes, that many
men should enjoy civil rights and be denied political
rights, that the enjoyment of both by the multitude
was in glaring contradiction to the pronounced
gradations between class and class and man and man,
as these are to be found in human nature all the
world over. 'Men,' he roundly declares, 'have no
right to what is not reasonable, and to what is not
for their benefit.' [1]

A similar conclusion followed from his conception
of society. Civil government is not called into being
as a mere instrument for realising rights already
possessed. It has a larger scope. It is 'an institution of beneficence.' It is 'made for the advantage
of man.' [2] And it fulfils this beneficent task, not
by a wholesale enactment of codes or declarations of
rights fashioned in abstraction for Utopia, but by
the gradual realisation of those conditions of civilised
life which can be won only by degrees, and by the
labours of successive generations. Amongst these
conditions are some so fundamental, some which
so manifestly lie upon the very threshold of social
well-being, that the happiness of a people demands
that they should be secured by law. Such are the
ordinary civil rights of a well-constituted state.
But Burke does not limit his view to these. He

[1] *Reflections.*   [2] *Ibid.*

even goes so far as to venture, and to repeat, the sweeping assertion that 'all the advantages for which civil society is established become man's right.'[1]   'Whatever each man can separately do,' so he runs on in expanding this dictum, 'without trespassing on others, he has a right to do for himself ; and he has a right to a fair portion of all which society, with all its combinations of skill and force, can do in his favour.'[2]   But having said this, he is quick to add that the right to political power is another matter.   Conceivably, this too might be one of the advantages that are rights.   For this 'right' is not to be dogmatically and *a priori* repudiated any more than dogmatically and *a priori* admitted.   The whole question is ruled by convention and convenience, and these are always conditioned by circumstances.   Yet two points emerge with perfect clearness.   The one, that in society as he conceives it, a share in political power, authority, and direction, is not an essential ; or (as he phrases it) not one of 'the direct original rights of man in civil society' : the other, that in the particular civil societies which were more especially before his eyes, France and England, the right to the franchise was, in his estimate, so far from being an advantage, either to its possessor or to his country, that it was much more likely to produce a social cataclysm.   Hence, as we have already

[1] *Reflections.*   [2] *Ibid.*

seen, Burke is as firm in denying political rights
to all except the comparatively few who have the
capacity for exercising them, as he is in recognising
the civil rights that are indispensable for all. And
his grounds for the denial are equally his grounds
for the recognition. Needless to repeat that they
are not to be found in his recognition of abstract
natural rights. He admits, as always, that these
exist. But they appear only to make it evident
how small a part they play in settling what rights
ought to be given, and what claims to rights resisted,
in the actual politics of civil societies. ' The moment
you abate anything from the full rights of men
each to govern himself, and suffer any artificial
positive limitation upon those rights, from that
moment the whole organisation of government
becomes a consideration of convenience.' [1] And
what ' convenience ' dictates—a thing most difficult
to compute—is only to be determined in the light
of a comprehensive conception of the happiness of
the people as an organic whole.

Burke's attitude to abstract rights appears therefore to be this. He explicitly affirms that abstract
rights exist ; he even specifies what some of these
purely abstract rights are (the right *e.g.* of self-
defence). But he sets little value upon any attempt
to formulate these rights at length in a code of
rights applicable to all places and all times. He

[1] *Reflections.*

prefers to concentrate his attention upon such rights as can and ought to be enjoyed by ' the civil social man, and no other.' And the point he here insists upon is that rights must always be relative to the human nature of the persons who claim to enjoy them, and to the constitution of the social system in which they are to be enjoyed. By doing this he shakes himself free from the dogmatism of the authors of purely abstract codes of the rights of man, and commits himself to the position that all rights with which statesmen (as contrasted with theorists) are concerned, must be made good by argument and proof. In this respect he is at one with Bentham. For it is one of the most valuable features of both Bentham and Burke that, as against the dogmatism of Paine and his allies, they insist on proof. On the other hand, however, he escapes the untenable narrowness of Bentham ; for the existence of a right, as he conceives it, does not rest on its legal enactment, nor even on the mere political utility that justifies enactment in Benthamite eyes. Utility comes in : it comes in inasmuch as the happiness of the people is recognised as the supreme end. But as there neither is, nor ever can be, any such thing as the happiness of a people which does not include the conservation of the prescriptive experience of the past, and not least of prescriptive rights (which were less than nothing to Bentham), it is obvious that the kind of proof that would satisfy Bentham would not by any means satisfy Burke. He is not minded to brush the past aside, nor count it as of no account that a right has been long acknowledged and enjoyed. Nor is he in the least disposed to regard the claim to a right not hitherto enjoyed (the right to the franchise, for example) as either just or reasonable, in the absence of proof that it could be grafted on the gradually developed organic unity of the body-politic.

There is a sense in which this conservative caution in the handling of rights is undoubtedly to be deplored. We have seen that Burke set little value on the dogma of the rights of man, with its codes and declarations. We have seen that, as against it, he concentrated his interest upon the civil social man and no other. But there was nothing in either of these things to have prevented him, had he been so minded, from giving the world some general scheme of the rights to which human nature, being what it is, might reasonably aspire under the normal conditions of civilised social life. For, so far from being out of harmony with his avowal that the centre of his interest was ' the civil social man and no other,' such an enterprise would only have been a discourse on the rights of the civil social man as he ought to be, and might hope to be, in the gradual evolution of a nation's life. It would, in other words, have been a theory of social rights. Nor, with his insight into human nature and his grasp of social conditions, was any man better fitted to execute such a task. This, however, is but an idle wish. His hostility to abstraction in any shape and form was too inveterate. His inclinations did not lie in that direction. His career plunged him deep into the concrete and the practical. And he had early developed a distrust of all plans and projects, and still more of all theories divorced from immediate conditions of place and time. Hence his relegation of all discussion of abstract rights ' to the schools.' Hence his refusal to discuss what is not rigorously practical. Hence his disposition to rest on rights that are real, because sanctioned by law, prescription, and consensus, in preference to the rights that are still in the region of innovating claim and argument. Yet here, as elsewhere, we meet the usual result. In arguing against theory he himself theorises, and in resisting the radical claim to this or that specific right, he is led on to define the conditions upon which rights in general ought to be conceded or withheld. Hence the fruitfulness of his pages even for the reader whose interest in rights is purely theoretical. That rights are not to be dogmatised but proved : that all discussion of rights must recognise the nature of man and the constitution of civil society : that the real (not the merely hypothetical) rights of man are not mysterious gifts of nature which the individual needs only to be born in order to possess :

that, on the contrary, they are ' advantages,' or (as we might prefer to say) opportunities which the beneficent action of society and government gradually wins for the members of a community, that each may fulfil the duties of his station to man and to God : that if rights are to be given, or denied, gift or denial must derive from the happiness of the people as an organic whole : that no rights are to be more jealously guarded than those which by ' the discipline of nature ' have been woven into the constitution of a people—these, with the reasons annexed, are Burke's legacy to the theorist about rights.

The value of the legacy, and not least the demand for proof, is unimpeachable. It is so easy to call a desire, or even a greed, if only it be sufficiently strong, or a claim if only it be sufficiently confident, a right without its really being so, that a thinker in politics can hardly render a more needed service than to point out the conditions which must be satisfied before a demand, however passionately pressed, can become a right that can justly be demanded. No student of Burke's pages is likely ever again to fall into the ' anarchic fallacy,' as Bentham dubbed it, of confusing an inclination with a right. For to Burke, as to Bentham, all rights, in so far as they are substantial,[1] are not ultimate but derivative. Their justification is possible, not because they are

[1] The qualifying clause is necessary because, of course, the abstract and empty ' rights of uncovenanted man,' which Burke affirms (p. 196), are obviously original and not derivative.

original, self-evident, incapable of further proof, but because they can be shown to be conducive to the happiness of a people as this is construed in the light of the facts and laws of human nature and social existence. Nor is it a bad description of a right—though philosophers would doubtless wish to push the description to definition—to say, as in effect Burke says, that it is a position of ' advantage ' in which, as member of a civil society, the ' political animal ' man either actually is, or ought to be secured, especially by law and prescription, in order that he may contribute to the happiness of his country by fulfilling the duties of his divinely allotted station.

Nor, it may be added, are rights in Burke's eyes any the less ' natural ' because they are the rights of a highly civilised society. There is more than one passage in which he refuses, as stoutly as Aristotle, to identify the natural with the primitive, or to regard mankind as more natural, in proportion as they are less developed. For, though the rights which the members of a well-developed state enjoy are in a sense artificial, being as they are the product of the political art by which the constitution of a state is slowly fashioned, it is equally true that, as Burke himself reminds us, ' Art is man's nature,' and that nature is never more truly herself than in her grandest forms.' [1] And if this be sound, it

[1] See p. 53.

follows obviously that there can be no rights more truly natural, because none more truly characteristic of human nature at its best, than the rights enjoyed in a civil society. The point may seem to some no more than a matter of words. And it may be admitted, to the relief of the reader, that it is undesirable to stir the controversies that have raged around ' nature ' and ' natural.' None the less it may serve to suggest how decisively Burke set the rights of the citizen above the ' natural ' rights with which the protagonists of the rights of man were so ready to endow even the savage who, whatever be his other endowments, knows nothing either of the enabling advantages or the advantageous restraints of civilisation.

(b) *Rights and Circumstances*

Burke's contribution to the subject of rights is, however, by no means limited to thus suggesting a criterion by which the rights that are reasonable and real may be distinguished from the ' rights ' that are false and fanatical. Many of the greatest, and some of the best known, of his pages are given to the further, and hardly less interesting, question of the justice and expedience of enforcing rights even when their existence is not in dispute.

This is best illustrated by his attitude on the fateful quarrel between the mother country and the American colonies. For readers of his pregnant

words on the American crisis—Lord Morley goes
so far as to call them ' the most perfect manual
in our literature, or in any literature, for one who
approaches the study of public affairs, whether for
knowledge or for practice ' [1]—will not find him
either denying the existence of the abstract right
of the mother country to tax the colonies,[2] or
affirming the abstract right of the colonists as individuals to resist the obnoxious taxation. Putting
the question of the right of taxation ' totally out
of the question,' he pleads for the necessity of
raising the whole controversy to a higher level, and
urges, with an extraordinary persuasiveness, that
the possession of an abstract constitutional right,
however well grounded, is far from justifying the
policy of asserting and enforcing that right up to
the hilt. In the name of ' prudence,' that mother
of all the political virtues, such a thing is not to
be so much as thought of. For the vital matter in
a political crisis is not what a political lawyer tells
us *may* be done ; it is what humanity, justice, and
expediency tell us *ought* to be done under the concrete conditions of the given case. Nor does he
hesitate to affirm that the consciousness of having
an abstract right in one's favour is so far from
furnishing a justification for exercising it, that it
ought to make its possessor peculiarly careful lest,

---

[1] *Burke*, p. 81, in ' English Men of Letters.'

[2] On the contrary he was quite prepared to affirm it *as an
abstract principle*.

in exacting his right, he may be perpetrating an
oppressive and disastrous wrong. This runs throughout. With a grasp of the situation beyond any
man of his time, he argues that the practical insistence on the right to tax is to the last degree
irrational and, in a deeper than the legal sense,
unjust. From first to last his eyes, like those of
the utilitarians after him, are fixed on the public
good, and to him, as to them, the happiness of the
people (though in his own sense of the word) is
paramount in politics. Nor would he suffer a single
right, no matter what constitutional authorities
could be cited in its favour, to become the basis of
action, till it had proved its claim to descend from
the parchments of constitutional lawyers into the
concrete realities and expediencies of practical
politics. It is here in short that he stands forward,
in what is probably his best known character, as the
great apologist of ' circumstances '—circumstances
which impose upon all rights whatsoever their inevitable and, rightly looked at, their reasonable
limitations and abatements. ' Sir, I think you
must perceive that I am resolved this day to have
nothing at all to do with the question of the right
of taxation. . . . It is less than nothing in my
consideration. . . . My consideration is narrow,
confined, and wholly limited to the policy of the
question. . . . The question with me is, not whether
you have a right to render your people miserable,

but whether it is not your interest to make them happy. It is not what a lawyer tells me I *may* do ; but what humanity, reason, and justice tell me I ought to do.' [1] 'What is the use,' he elsewhere asks, 'of discussing a man's abstract right to food or medicine ? The question is upon the method of procuring and administering them.' Call in the farmer and physician, not the professor of metaphysics. [2]

The sanity of these sentences, and of many others like them, was, of course, proved by the event. Deaf to Burke's counsels, England tried to enforce a right and lost a continent. But this is not our present concern. The point is that, in these and all similar utterances, Burke once and for all exposed the folly of all policy, from whatever source it may emanate, that takes its stand upon rights, and shuts its eyes to those larger considerations by which the enforcement of any right, public or private, individual or corporate, ought always in the name of the public good to be qualified, restrained, and regulated. It is not that rights in law may not exist, nor that they may not have to be enforced. Burke would be the last person to dispute it. No writer in our language has a profounder respect for law. All that he insists upon, with a passionate reasonableness, is the need for proof—proof that the enforcement of a right, or the refusal to enforce a right, is justified under existing

[1] Speech on Conciliation with America.   [2] *Reflections.*

circumstances in the highest interests of the nation as a whole.

The same attitude repeats itself in the handling of the rights of individuals. When Price, in his sermon,[1] tabulated his version of the fundamental rights of the citizen, one of these was the right to resist power where abused. Burke does not deny the right, even though it may carry in its train the dire necessity of dethroning a king. How could he ? Was he not a Whig ? Neither did he doubt that this formidable right of resistance might, in emergency, have to be translated into acts of resistance and even of revolution. For, as a Whig, he was not likely to repudiate the men of 1688 and their deeds, however anxious he is to pare these down to 'a revolution not made but prevented.' But, then, there comes the characteristic reminder that the step from abstract right of resistance to concrete act of resistance is not to be taken without convincing evidence that the situation is so dire and deplorable as to justify resort to this extreme medicine of distempered commonwealths. And, least of all, was such a doctrine to be cried on the housetops by men such as (much too rashly it must be confessed) he took Price and his friends to be—men 'who have nothing of politics but the passions they excite.' 'The question of dethroning kings,' he says, in guarded phrase, 'will always

[1] The sermon referred to in the *Reflections*.

be a question of dispositions and of means, and of probable consequences rather than of positive rights. As it was not made for common abuses, so it is not to be agitated by common minds. The speculative line of demarcation where obedience ought to end, and resistance must begin, is faint, obscure, and not easily definable. It is not a single act or a single event which determines it.' [1]

This reminder, this reasonable plea for caution and proof in the exercise of rights, is never out of date. Fanatics for rights are to be found in all civilised communities. The world seems never weary of producing them. Nor are they less fanatical when the rights they press to extremes are entirely legal. For this makes them only the more formidable, as giving them a solid, *i.e.* a legal, ground for their immoderation. They number in their ranks the strainers of prerogative, the zealots for the rights of legislatures and governments, the protagonists for orders and institutions, the irreconcilables who press the rights of individual liberty against authority or the rights of authority against the individual conscience, not to say the pernicious pedants who push to the letter of the law ' the right to do what they will with their own.' Such traffickers in extremes are not to be met by challenging their rights. This cannot silence them. It only exasperates them into an even more extravagant

[1] *Reflections.*

assertion of rights which are, or may be, indubitably legal. It only confirms them in the fallacy that their immoderation is justice because it gives them an opportunity of appealing to ' justice ' in their immoderation. The truly effective line of attack is Burke's : it is to bid them, in the name of sanity, think less of what, in the letter, is just, and more of what, on the actual merits of the situation, is humane and public-spirited. To vary the phrase, it is to tell them that it is a poor tribute to the cause of rights to forget that there are duties and utilities towards the public good, by which the exercise of all rights, however justifiable in the eye of the law, must always be qualified and controlled.

Such, in brief, are Burke's main contributions to a doctrine of rights. As may now be evident, they fall under two heads. Under the first, he discusses what rights can be legitimately claimed by the members of a given civil society ; and the point that emerges here, with utmost clearness, is that he was always convinced that the rights enjoyable under law and government, the rights of ' the civil social man,' are immeasurably more valuable and substantial than any ' primitive ' rights (and, as we have seen, he recognises such) which mankind may have to surrender to secure them. Under the second head, he preaches his doctrine of ' circumstances,' with its perpetual refrain that it is sheer

folly and fanaticism to turn a right into an ultimatum. ' There is no arguing,' he once said, ' with
these fanatics of the rights of man.' No, there was
no arguing with them, because having made up
their minds that to have a right and to press for its
realisation forthwith were one and the same thing,
they seemed to have shut their ears to those larger
considerations of humanity, justice, and expediency
which the practical wisdom of the statesman is
bound, in the name of the happiness of the people,
to recognise.

Hence it is easy to understand his antagonism to
the dogma of the equality of men which was commonly
put in the forefront of the revolutionary declarations
of rights. His position here may be summed up
in his own formula : ' All men have equal rights,
but not to equal things.'[1] Needless to say, it does
not mean that all men either have, or ought to have,
the same rights. For, as we have seen, it was of the
essence of his theory of government that political
rights were, or ought to remain, in the enjoyment
of the few. The dictum therefore means no more
than that, once rights are given, those who enjoy
them must be equal in the eye of the law. We have
seen how far he was prepared to go—even to blood—
in defence of the civil rights even of the poorest.[2]
And yet these equal rights are never ' rights to
equal things.' They are only opportunities (' ad-

[1] *Reflections.*   [2] P. 171.

vantages,' as he called them) upon which as basis endless inequalities may be developed. For, as it is beyond doubt that men are born into the world with all degrees of personal inequalities which cling to them throughout, it is inevitable that, in the sifting struggle of life, some make more of their opportunities than others. By dint of vital energy, force of character, and the incidents of that happy chance which can never be eliminated, they stand above their fellows on the strength of achieved superiorities which equality of civil rights—and we may add equality of political rights (though Burke would have none of it)—can do comparatively little to level. This was his consistent attitude. The same line of thought that led him to his *apologia* for a ' natural aristocracy ' in his handling of government, has its natural sequel in the conclusion, that whatever be the equal rights which the citizens of a State enjoy, these equal rights are not, and never can be, rights to equal things. Equality of rights, however far it may legitimately be pressed, remains at best no more than the foundation of those many modes of inequality ' without which there is no nation.'

CHAPTER XI

(a) *The Unity of the State*

IT is safe to assume that no one, in the light of what
the nineteenth century has done for political thought,
is likely to quarrel with Burke for insisting that
the great ' partnership ' of society is an organic
unity. This is his merit, and the very ground on
which it has been so justly said that he was far in
advance of his age. There still, however, remains
an opening for criticism. For there is certainly
room for the suggestion that, as conceived by him,
society is not organic enough, and that it is not
organic enough, because it is not sufficiently democratic.

There are doubtless quarters in which a criticism
such as this, and in especial the last clause of it,
is not likely to command assent. Obviously enough
it conflicts with a notion which, since the dawn of
political thought in Greece, has again and again
come to the front, and not only in the camps of
conservatism—the familiar doctrine, namely, that
democracy makes for disintegration. And this, it
may be admitted, is, in a sense, undeniably true.

For beyond gainsaying, democracy, in all its greatest exponents, stands for the claims of individual free choice. This is of its essence. And from this it is no great step to the suspicion, and the fear, that it is very certain to become a corrosive, if not a deadly solvent of all those ties between ruler and subject, class and class, man and man, which rest upon authority, custom, and prescription. For is it not inevitable that, as the claims of individual free choice push their way, as indeed they must, into the theory and practice of liberty of thought, discussion, and action, there must needs be an end of the unsuspecting confidence and unquestioning loyalty with which the social rank and file, in the days before democracy comes to trouble the waters, accept the laws and institutions of the State as not to be called in question ? Nor is it in the least doubtful that there is a world of difference between the ages of Status and the ages of Choice ; or (in less technical phrase) between that condition of things, so dear to the reverent mind of Burke, in which the situation of the individual is the arbiter of his duties, and that vastly altered democratic dispensation under which the choice of the individual would fain make itself the arbiter of his situation. Momentous indeed is the transition. Nor is the step likely to be taken by any people without social and political upheavals which transform society to its foundations. Small wonder therefore if conservative minds, with whom, as with Burke, it is an article of faith that ties are not lightly to be broken, should come to dread and denounce the coming of democracy, as if it meant the destruction of all that they and their forefathers have most valued, and even as the dissolution of the bonds and ligaments that hold society together. Such, at any rate, has been the burden of the indictment of democracy from the days when Plato [1] satirised the democratic licence that masquerades in the guise of liberty to our own times, when Carlyle derided ' nomadic contract,' bewailed the rupture of all ties except ' cash nexus,' scoffed at the ' liberty—to leap over precipices,' and roundly declared that there was ' no longer any social idea extant.' [2] Such also is substantially the indictment we find in Burke, who was, as we have seen, convinced that, were the radicalism of the rights of man suffered to run its course, it would disintegrate the State, and dissolve the great partnership of civil society into the dust and powder of individualism.

Nor is it for any one, however strong his democratic sympathies, to deny that these disasters might happen. In political changes nothing can obviate risks. It is beyond a doubt that disintegrating forces not a few exist and operate within democracy. In many ways democracy divides. There are individualists whose atomistic creed is

[1] *Republic*, Bk. viii.   [2] *Sartor Resartus.*

the negation of all government, and collectivists who are the terror of individualists. There are dissenters from dissent, and irreconcilable groups and parties which are the torment and despair of statesmen; and not least there is the menacing clash of economic interests. And these are natural enough. Every type of political system has its own perversion, and it is reasonable enough to think that the perversion of democracy lies towards anarchy. Yet there is neither reason nor justice in judging any form of polity by its perversions actual or possible. These may have their place as warnings and danger signals. But they are no more sufficient ground for an ultimate judgment than are the possible or even actual vices of an individual for a final estimate of his character. It is better therefore, and fairer, to judge of democracy and its tendencies in the light of its ideal and the forces it has at its command for translating that ideal into fact. And if it be so judged, it is hardly rash to say that it is so far from making for social disintegration, as its foes aver, that of all political types it is the one which by its very nature makes for organic unity.

For when is a civil society in the fullest sense organic? Obviously it is when the institutions it gathers up within it, and the orders or classes of which it consists, stand related in that peculiarly intimate fashion which has driven political thinkers to indulge so freely in biological analogies. But, then, these institutions and orders do not hang together of themselves. The bond that binds them into unity, as these biological analogies imply, is life. And though, of course, we may often enough talk of the life or soul or spirit of a people or nation, it is difficult to see what this 'soul' is, or where it resides, if it be not as actualised in the lives of the men and women of whom a people or nation must needs consist. Where is the soul of a mill when its looms are deserted, of a shipyard when its hammers are silent, of a ship in dock, of a club when it has closed its doors, of a homestead abandoned to dilapidation, of a city (if in these days we can imagine such a thing) from which its inhabitants have fled ? That a society is made up of individuals may be a false, or at any rate a halting, statement. It must be a halting statement, if it fails to do justice to the fact that the substance and content, the interests, ideas, activities, which make the individual life worth living, come into it in and through the feeding and fostering actualities of the social environment. To become an individual, in the true and not merely atomistic sense of the word, a man must have already lived in organic union with his fellows. Else would the social group, be it family, village, city, or nation, lapse into a mere aggregate or mass of units which is no longer really a society. All this may be conceded. Yet, when we press the question, when and in what form these organic ties, which count for so much, are to be found, where can they be found elsewhere than in the lives of the actual men and women, the *persons* in the fullest sense of the word, who generation after generation, vitalise the institutions of a people by throwing in their lot with them, and by instinctively, habitually, purposefully giving such force as they possess to the work of the community ? For, however true it may be, and it is indisputably true, that the life of a city or a nation (not to speak of many lesser groups) is an infinitely larger thing than the life of any individual, or any group of individuals, within it ; however undeniable it may be, and it is undeniable, that the citizens of city or state are always being led on to results greater than, or at any rate other than, those they anticipate, so that their destinies may seem to be controlled by a larger will and plan, this does not alter the fact that there is one condition without which that larger will and wider plan would be reduced to impotence ; and that condition is the striving and effort, be it instinctive or deliberate, of actual human beings in whom the breath of social life must needs be found, if it is to be found anywhere. Always the unity, fitly called organic, of every social group, from the least to the greatest, is strong and real, and not merely nominal or notional, in proportion as the ends or interests for which the group stands, are reflected

and actualised in the lives of its members.   For this
is of the essence of social vitality in all its modes.

We can see this clearly enough in some of the
lesser groups.   What, for example, is a united
family, if it be not one in which the family traditions,
the family fortunes, the family hopes, sorrows, interests, ambitions are shared, up to the limits of
their several capacities, by every one within its
well-knit circle ?   What is a prosperous institution,
be it club, trades-union, church, university, political party, or what not, if it be not one that is
instinct with life, because everything that seriously
concerns the institution as a whole, its objects, its
management, its reputation, its plan and policy, is
likewise the serious concern of even the least of its
members ?   Institutions, no doubt, may sometimes
continue to exist—history is strewn with the wrecks
of them—long after the life has gone out of them.
They may endure, though they can hardly be said to
survive, when they no longer live in the lives and
loyalties of their members.   In name, or in law, or
in tradition, or in outward appearance, they may
still possess a kind of unity.   But such have no
longer an *organic* unity, because they have ceased
to be a meeting-point of human feelings and wills,
united in a partnership for the furtherance of those
common ends and interests which that partnership
is designed to subserve.   For institutions live their
real life in the lives of men or not at all.   Apart from

this, they may have a local habitation and a name ; they may have imposing adjuncts and officials and endowments, and a record that goes far into the past. But they have no longer organic unity, because none of these things have life, if there be no lives to vitalise them. There is no future before any institution, if it be not, as generation succeeds generation, born again and ever again in the souls of its members.

So with the great comprehensive institution, the State. Needless to say that it gathers up within it many ends and many interests. Needless to add that these ends and interests are so many and so multifarious that there is room and to spare for unlimited division of energy and effort in their pursuit and enjoyment. So much so, that to expect that each member should actively participate in all would be an extravagant absurdity. This group or that, this class or that, will, of course, always have its own peculiar concerns, into which it turns the central currents of its energies ; though it will always be found, on closer inspection, that even the most sectional, fractional, or selfish of these have, without exception, their far-reaching social significance. Yet clearly enough there are ends and interests that are salient and paramount. We may call them common, public, collective, national, imperial. And we rightly say that a civil society has risen towards organic unity in proportion as its members, whilst not neglectful of the

narrower ties, are in their wills and loyalties enlisted in the service of those larger ends of which
the civilised State is the bearer and the sponsor.
And from this it follows that, if it should happen,
by the exigencies, accidents, or apathies of the
national history, that there are within the community groups or classes who do not, up to the
limits of their capacities, participate in those paramount ends for which a State exists, then that community must still fall short of organic unity in the
full sense of the conception. Failing this, it may
still be strong, so strong that it may present a secure
and formidable front to other nations. For an
autocracy enthroned on helotage has done this
before now. And it may also, within itself (for
otherwise it could not be strong), be far from loosely
knit in the system of its institutions. But the ties
and ligaments, the ' spiritual bond ' of feeling, will,
and aim, will still be wanting, so long as there remains a sharp dividing-line between groups and
classes who genuinely participate in the paramount
ends of national life and the groups and classes who,
for one reason or another, are debarred from identi-
fying their wills and fidelities with these. A slave
state may be great ; the slave states of the ancient
world were great ; but no state can be fitly called
one and organic, so long as it contains even any
considerable minority of men who have little or no
share in those large and supremely valuable ends

and interests for which it is the glory, as it is also the responsibility, of the nation to stand. For these ends and interests will not be the meeting-point of the hopes, the fears, the pride, the effect, the ideals, of all its citizens.

Now this is what, in its ideal at any rate, the democratic state seeks and hopes to remedy. It may, of course, fall short. In many ways, and for many reasons, democracy, like every other form of polity may, and indeed must, fail of its ideal. The imperious urgencies of foreign policy, the exigencies of increasing and even of perpetually reproducing the national wealth, the intellectual or moral back-wardness of its population, the weight of national tradition and habit, the political apathy which makes people content to be law-abiding subjects rather than good citizens—these are some of the many obstructions that defeat the hopes of the impatient prophets of democracy. But wherever the democratic spirit is alive, these things are not frustrations : they are only hindrances. For demo-cracy is more, and deeper than a predilection for a form of government, though Sir Henry Maine has tried to narrow it down to that.[1] Burke had a truer insight when he said—and it was one of the reasons why he feared it—that the Revolution was akin to a religious and proselytising movement. For the democratic movement that has run its course

[1] In his *Popular Government*.

during the past century has almost always found its inspiration in certain convictions about the claims and the worth of the individual, which will not suffer those who hold them to rest till they have won for all orders and classes the opportunity of effective participation in the political life of the State. This has been the democratic aim, as it is already to no small extent the democratic achievement. And the justification both of aim and achievement lies, not merely in security against irresponsible power, nor yet in the well-worn argument that a democratic constitution brings public interests well worth living for into private lives which otherwise would be lamentably narrowed, but in the contention that there is no surer path to national strength than that which leads towards a national unity which is truly organic because none are left outside of it. The truism, so true of many forms of social organisation from the family onwards, that strength comes of unity, is surely also true of the nation.

But this, it must be evident, is not the kind of unity we find in Burke. When he speaks of the well-compacted fabric of justice cramped and bolted together in all its parts, the picture that rises is that of the unity of a people in his own sense of the word. It is the idea of a people as it comes into being by ' the discipline of nature,' differenti-ated into many ranks, classes, orders, functions, and permeated through and through with the spirit of

inequality. And as the fact of inequality is nowhere more unimpeachable than in disparities of
political capacity, the result to which he comes is
not a truly organic, but a bisected state. On the
one side of the dividing-line stands his 'natural
aristocracy' supported by a close electorate and a
limited 'British public';[1] on the other the great
mass of the population, who, whatever be the worth
of their private lives, are shut out, by inherent
incapacity, from political rights and functions. This,
to be sure, need not be *fatal* to the unity of a people.
For society, as Burke has told us,[2] is a partnership
in much besides political institutions in the narrower
sense of the words. Nor is it to be forgotten that
Burke always thinks of the unenfranchised multitude as united with all their fellow-countrymen in
a common patriotism. He is far from claiming
patriotism as the monopoly of the privileged electorate, or even of his 'British public.' Yet the cleavage
remains. For the 'partnership' of his glowing
words can never be so complete, nor can the unity
he glorified be so organic, so long as there is a mass
of men within the State, in whom political interests
and activities do not join hands with the many
other less public ends for which they live. The
result follows. Despite all those eloquent words
about the 'great partnership,' and (we might add)
despite the shining example Burke's own career

[1] P. 163. [2] P. 59.

affords of the extent to which the ends for which
the nation stands can saturate the life of a citizen,
the State as he conceives it falls asunder, disrupted
into the few who share political power, and the
many whose humble rôle it is to be ' the objects of
protection or the means of force.' It is aristocratic
to the core ; and because it is so aristocratic it is
so much the less organic. Hence it is not too much
to say that Burke's conception of society fails just
where it is strongest. Its strength lies in its insistence, so eloquent, so convincing, on the unity of the
whole : the weakness is that the unity is not
complete.

This line of criticism, however, it is safe to say,
would have made no impression upon Burke. He
was too firmly convinced that the breaking up of
political power into the multitudinous fragments of
a widely extended franchise was the straight road
to anarchy. And this conviction, from which he
never wavered, was not the child of prejudice. As
we have seen in the chapter on government, it rested
on twin supports : on his plea for ' a natural aristocracy,' and on his settled estimate of the political
incapacity of the multitude, whom he so decisively
ruled out of all share in political power. It rested,
in short, on the doctrine of Whig trusteeship. And
to this we may now turn.

There is a way of dealing with this aristocratic
doctrine of Whig trusteeship that is all too easy.

Burke, it has been said, died protesting against the inevitable ; and the inevitable has come. Whig trusteeship has, beyond question, been overthrown in practical politics. And if so, what need for further refutation ? Is this *solvitur ambulando* not enough, now that a century and more has gone by ? Nay, has not Burke himself told us that the course of history is nothing less than ' the known march of the providence of God ' ? A thousand years may be as one day in the eye of God, but the verdict of a century must surely count for much in the life of a nation as seen by the eyes of men.

This, however, is far from enough. It is needful to remember that the mere fact that a great political movement has beaten down its opponents on the plains of recent history is no sufficient proof that it has won in argument. Even if we believe, with Schiller and Hegel, that the history of the world is the judgment of the world, this memorable dictum is not to be applied except over large stretches of Time. And even if it be argued, as well it may, that the case for any social system is weakened by the lapse of years during which its reformers hold their ground, and thereby become themselves after a fashion prescriptive, it does not follow that, theoretically, at any rate, we are justified in adding it to the forlorn catalogue of lost causes, till we are satisfied that it has yielded ground before something more rational than what may after all be nothing

more than the blind push of brute natural forces.
Democracy victorious may be a different thing from
democracy justified. The argument from success is
premature. The democracies of Europe are, in
fact, still new to their work, and are still upon their
trial. And when we turn to their publicists and
prophets, we find them sharply at variance. Individualists are, to say the least, suspicious of socialists;
and socialists, to say no more, impatient of individualists. Utilitarianism has long ago, to its own
complete satisfaction, demolished the radical dogma
of the natural rights of man ; and Herbert Spencer,
in his turn, hating socialism with a perfect hatred,
has denounced the Benthamite faith in the omnipotence of the majority as a political superstition.
Meanwhile the foes of democratic government have
not been silent. Carlyle has satirised it with a
derisive humour unequalled since Plato. Sir Henry
Maine, from a world-wide survey of institutions,
old and new, has pronounced it to be to the last
degree fragile, and to be densely impervious to the
light of ideas—except the light, *not* from Heaven,
of the ' broken-down theories of Rousseau and
Bentham.' And the naturalism of our day, in
some of its prophets at any rate, is greatly more
concerned to laud and magnify ' the superman '
than to hold a brief on any terms for humble worth
and the democratic rank and file, who, if Nietzsche
is to be believed, are good for nothing but to swell

statistics. Even John Stuart Mill, radical and optimist though he was, caught up the note of alarm from De Tocqueville's *Democracy in America*, and sounded a warning blast against the menace of that multiplied tyranny of the multitude which made him the champion of enlightened minorities. With facts like these in view, it is permissible to think that, if Burke's theory of government is to be laid on the shelf, it ought to be in deference to other arguments than the dubious 'logic of accomplished facts.' It has still a claim to be examined on its merits. And as it involves two salient points, the affirmation of the political incapacity of the multitude and the plea for a 'natural aristocracy,' we may, as matter of arrangement, take these in turn.

(b) *The Political Incapacity of the Multitude*

It is possible that, upon this fundamental point, Burke's convictions may have a historical justification. Let historians decide. It is for them to say, from an exact and intimate knowledge of the English people in the latter half of the eighteenth century, if Burke was wrong, and if Pitt, not to say Shelburne and Richmond (who went much further) were right in advocating large measures of enfranchisement. Our concern is with Burke's arguments only in so far as they have been generalised, as they have often been, into a case against the democratic movement of the nineteenth century and the democratic reforms which have followed in its train. Are the friends of democracy in a position to say that these arguments have been refuted ? Can they specify where their weakness lies ? This is the challenge which must be met.

The challenge is, however, one which democracy need not fear to face. For there is one aspect at any rate in which Burke has made the case for his uncompromising exclusions difficult by nothing so much as by his own admissions. For his vein is not the vein of Coriolanus. The rabble, the mob, the common herd, the louts, the clowns, the rotten multitudinous canaille, and suchlike are not expletives characteristic of him. However bitter and envenomed the words he flung at the sanguinary proletariat of Paris—did he not call them ' a swinish multitude ' ? [1]—it was far enough from his large and sympathetic mind to think thus meanly and savagely of the great mass of his humble fellow-countrymen, for whose claims and virtues he had, as we have seen,[2] a sincerity of respect which many a radical might imitate. ' He censures God who quarrels with the imperfections of men.' Such was his avowed conviction ; and it is entirely in keeping with it that ' to love and respect his kind ' is one of the marks of the statesman after his own heart. But it is just this attitude of respect that goes far

[1] It was explained as evoked by the inhuman execution of Bailly, the historian of astronomy.
[2] P. 170.

to undermine his Whig exclusiveness. It gives the democratic critic an opening. For however wide the step from respecting a human being to the wish to give him a share in political power ; and however easy it be to point to men, even the best and the greatest, like Scott or Carlyle, who have exalted the peasant saint and abhorred the democratic voter, it is none the less the fact that there is no idea, not even liberty or fraternity, more fundamentally fatal to all political monopolies and exclusions than the idea and sentiment of respect for men. Nor is it difficult to see why. For when one man genuinely respects another, it is never merely because of what that other may have actually succeeded in making of himself and his opportunities ; it is, always in part and sometimes mainly, because he believes that the person he respects has capacities and powers which, given more favouring conditions, would find fuller realisation. If it be just and right to estimate mankind by what they are, we can never value them at their real worth, if we do not include in what they are, the something more, be it much or little, which they have it in them to become. This comes to light quite clearly, it is in fact a commonplace, in all those cases where human faculty and promise are manifestly obstructed by disease, penury, or ill-fortune. Nor do we go one whit beyond the facts in venturing the assertion that the very nerve of social effort would be cut, were it to happen that the more helpful and vigorous members of a community were convinced—could such a disaster befall them—that the mass of their fellow-citizens were inherently incapable of rising towards the opportunities of a happier lot and a larger life. To believe men to be worth helping implies some faith that they will respond to what is done for them. And if this is true even of the social stratum, where latent powers and capacities are at a minimum, it holds with incomparably greater force where these are normal, and by consequence more capable of response to larger opportunities.

Doubtless these larger opportunities need not include politics. Fortunately for all of us, there are many other things to live for. It is equally true that Burke and Scott and Carlyle were right in holding that men might have much worth without votes, and that demagogues are extravagant when they speak as if enfranchisement is the one specific for lifting mankind out of a pit of degradation. But this is not conclusive. For the point in issue is not whether ordinary men may not have much in their lives to be thankful for, even though they have never seen the inside of a polling-booth or a political meeting, but whether, be their private and personal worth what it may, they do not possess likewise sufficient political faculty and promise to justify, for their own sake and their country's, their admission to citizenship. And once the question is raised in this form, the presumption lies not in favour of permanent exclusions but in the contrary direction. For the object of respect as between man and man is not mere qualities, not even shining qualities : it is character. It is, in other words, the principle of moral and social life which, however grievously it may be stunted and obstructed, is nevertheless discernible in every normal human soul ; and this central principle of life and worth is so far from being circumscribed within fixed and unyielding limits that, as a matter of common experience, it is often eagerly responsive to new openings and opportunities. It was a doctrine of some of the Greek philosophers that, if a man have one virtue he has all the virtues. So stated it is, as it was meant to be, a paradox ; but it is a paradox that embodies the truth, none more fundamental in ethics, that he who has virtue in those relationships in which he has been put to the proof has within him a principle of virtue which, if opportunity be given, will not fail to assert itself in other directions. In other and more concrete words, if an artisan or a peasant have principle enough to be a good father, a true friend, a helpful neighbour, a capable workman, a law-abiding subject, the presumption is in favour of his becoming likewise a reasonably good citizen, if opportunity to prove his quality be given him. To pay to

humble worth our tribute of respect, as Burke does ;
to say that its interests are sacred, as Burke does ;
to declare that we are ready to shed our blood on
its behalf, as Burke does ; and then to add that
it must on no account be admitted to political
power, as Burke does—this may well appear, as
indeed it is, something of a *non sequitur.* The
presumption lies the other way.

A presumption such as this, however, though it
may weigh with believers in democracy, could not
be expected to count for much (or for anything) with
Burke. He was too firmly committed to his conviction, from which he never swerved, of the permanent political incapacity of the multitude.

Now the question at issue here is not whether
political incapacity exists. It cannot be doubted
that it exists, and is likely to continue to exist, in
all communities over the face of the earth. It must
exist so long as ignorance, indifference, levity, reck-
lessness, and lack of common sense are found
amongst mankind. The truth is that it exists so
widely—and nature must bear some part of the
reproach—as quite to overpass the ordinary lines
of class distinctions, and to have its representatives
in all ranks, classes, or orders whatsoever. If many
a country cottager may be politically incapable, so
may many a well-born idler. If many an artisan
or small shopkeeper may be politically incapable,
so (though for different reasons) may be many a

votary of luxury or sport, of social excitement or
money. Never is it to be forgotten, in all controversies about democratic franchises, that political
incapacity is certainly not the monopoly of the class
or classes upon which the aristocratic system of Whig
trusteeship, especially in Burke's version of it, so
decisively bolts the door.

The point that is here in issue, therefore, does
not turn essentially on the presence or absence of
political incapacity as between class and class, but
on the less depressing and more pertinent inquiry
whether the classes whom the old Whigs, or even
the new Whigs, would exclude from power are so
conspicuously lacking in the credentials for citizenship as Burke supposed. ' How,' we have heard him
ask,[1] ' shall he get wisdom who holdeth the plough
and glorieth in the goad ; who driveth oxen and is
occupied in their labours ; and whose talk is of
bullocks ? ' It is a pertinent question, and one
that might easily be expanded. How can he get
wisdom who wields the pick-axe, and drives the
rivet, who works the engine and stands behind the
counter, or who spends his years in office, foundry,
or factory ? For this, of course, is the question to
which democracy has to find its answer. Burke's
answer we have seen. His answer seemingly is,
Never. He relegates them all to the wrong side of
his bisecting line. The franchise is for none of

[1] P. 170.

them ; and even if some of them might find a place
in his limited 'British public,' the vast majority are
dismissed as 'the objects of protection or the means
of force.'   What then is the answer of democracy ?

In the first place it claims that the multitude
whom Burke would exclude have some important
qualifications for citizenship which are, not of course
solely but in peculiar measure, their own.   It is
a mistake to assume that the arguments for citizenship are in all points in favour of those classes who
enjoy the indubitable advantages of social position,
wealth, education, and leisure.   Is it not something
that the less fortunate and less favoured (as they are
often called) have, on their side, one advantage that
counts for much ?   They have direct experience,
in their own lives and by constant association with
men of their own station, of some of the gravest
hardships, grievances, and possibly injustices, which
parliaments and ministries exist to remedy or extinguish.   They know, for example, what it is—
for in these latter days at any rate they can learn
by experience what it is—to have their children
saved from ignorance by the elementary school, or
safeguarded against the scourges of disease and
squalor by officers of public health.   They feel in-
stantly and in their homes the pinch of industrial
depression and commercial crises, or the bitter experiences of strikes and lock-outs.   It is probable

enough that they can recall cases of some they have known passing into the dreary degradation of pauperism. And they have perforce, and far more than their more prosperous fellow-countrymen, been brought into repulsive contiguity with the congested misery of great cities, and even with the still more repulsive spectacle of vice and crime. Nor ought it to be forgotten in this connection that, though they may concern themselves but little with international affairs or diplomatic action, it is more than likely that the circle of their acquaintance, possibly their own firesides, have furnished the men who fight this country's battles by land and sea.

Now of much of this Burke was well aware (though some of the experiences specified were of course beyond the horizon of his age). He had always an open mind and heart for the hardships, sufferings, and grievances of the multitude. Did he not declare that, if need arose, he would take his stand on the side of the poor, and shed his blood on their behalf ? But, then, he could not think that there was any necessary connection between the experience of hardships and grievances and the claim to be represented in the parliament with which some redress of grievances and some alleviation of hardships might be supposed to rest. Convinced that legislatures and governments can, after all, do comparatively little for human happiness, and firm in his Whig confidence in the actual and possible achievements of *virtual* representation, he was not only content but resolved to leave the multitude politically inarticulate. Nor is this inflexible exclusiveness in the least softened by that religious spirit which has sometimes led democratic thinkers—Mazzini, for example, or T. H. Green—to argue that if a man have worth in the eye of God, he ought to be allowed the opportunity of proving his worth in politics as in other things. Far from it. For Burke's thought, in this reference, moves far more amongst the consolations than the incentives of religion. Its message to the multitude, outside the pale of the constitution, is to reverence the powers that be, which are also the powers ordained of God ; and, should their lives be hard and unsatisfying, to seek in ' the final proportions of eternal justice ' the true consolations for the sorrows and sufferings of an imperfect earthly lot.[1]

It is here, however, that democracy parts company with him. Needless to say, it does not affirm so rash a proposition as that experience of grievances and hardships, and nothing more, qualifies for the franchise. It may even adopt with conviction the words of its adversary : ' Great distress has never hitherto taught, and whilst the world lasts it never will teach, wise lessons to any part of man-

[1] *Reflections.*

kind. Men are as much blinded by the extremes of misery as by the extremes of prosperity.' [1] Nor does it stand committed to the equally extravagant assertion that, because a human being is religious, he is therefore fit to exercise a vote. No. Yet it does insist that such experiences ought to count. They ought to count because those who live through them, whatever be their limitations otherwise, are likely to possess an intimate, because real and personal knowledge of social conditions which must be understood, if legislators and administrators are really to grasp the facts and needs of national life. Doubtless the experiences as they come to individuals may be limited and narrow enough. And, of course, there is much else in the life of a nation that lies quite outside of them. But they are none the less of undeniable importance, because, being widely shared, they concern the lives and destinies of multitudes.

For it is a mistake to regard representative government as if it aimed at nothing more than the representation of opinions, or as if it were no more than a passably good device for setting rival interests by the ears in an assembly of the nation, in the hope that out of the clash and conflict of discordant demands, the public good will somehow come by its own. Important though it be for the members of a constituency to have their opinions expressed,

[1] Letter to a Member of the National Assembly.

and their interests upheld by a man of their choice, it is not less important that they should find a representative who can sympathetically enter into their life-experiences, so that thus equipped he may be able, faithfully and with all the weight of fact, to lay these in their reality before the representative assembly of the nation. For the weaknesses of statesmen and legislators too often lie, not in failing to apprehend the social facts and movements which come within their ken, but in failing to apprehend these *in their real depth and significance*. Hence, indeed, the demand one sometimes meets that all classes and interests in the State—land, capital, labour, law, learning, army, navy, and so forth—should, so far as is compatible with the motley composition of constituencies, be represented by men of their own order. The demand is often impracticable ; and it easily degenerates into a narrow forgetfulness that the member for a mining or a commercial or agricultural centre is, as Burke once reminded his constituents, also a member of Parliament, and as such has much else to do besides the holding of a brief for his own constituents. Yet it is not unreasonable. To borrow words of Burke's own : ' The virtue, spirit, and essence of a House of Commons consists in its being the express image of the feelings of the nation.'[1] And *ceteris paribus*, it is always an advantage that

[1] *Thoughts on the Present Discontents.*

a representative should not only *know about* the life-experiences of his constituents, but know them, if not from personal initiation, yet with something of the intimacy and reality which they wear to those who have actually lived through them. For this, and nothing less than this, is one of the prime ends which representative institutions are meant to attain.

It is here most of all, more than in the voicing of opinions, more than in the championing of class interests (as the word is often understood) that the ' virtual ' representative of Whig trusteeship is at a disadvantage. In many ways he may be excellent; but the hardships and grievances, the feelings and hopes of the multitude are less likely to have justice done to them by him. Not from want of head or of heart—it is far from necessary to follow Bentham and James Mill in branding all virtual representatives as sinister self-seekers—but for the simpler reason that he is less likely to enter into the life-experiences of those he claims to represent than the man of their own choice who is bound to win their confidence in seeking their support. However capable as man of affairs, however honest in his patriotism, there will still be something lacking, so long as the unenfranchised mass have no effective means of articulately bringing home to him the realities of their lives and lot. Almost in his own despite, and very easily if he be not blessed with uncommon insight

and sympathy, he will fall into the attitude—not
unknown in Whig circles—of viewing the grievances
he would redress, the hardships he would ameliorate,
the life-experiences he would represent, from without and not from within. Nor can it be said that
even Burke is wholly exempt from this limitation.
There is a passage in Paine's *Rights of Man* in which
that mordant critic of the *Reflections* takes his enemy
to task : ' Nature,' he says, ' has been kinder to
Mr. Burke than he is to her. He is not affected by
the reality of distress touching his heart, but by the
showy resemblance of it striking his imagination.
He pities the plumage, but forgets the dying bird.
Accustomed to kiss the aristocratic hand that hath
purloined him from himself, he degenerates into a
composition of art, and the genuine soul of nature
deserts him. His hero or his heroine must be a
tragedy victim, expiring in show ; and not the real
prisoner of misery, sliding into death in the silence
of a dungeon.' The words are extravagant. The
estimate is false. And it would be easy to retort
that, when all is said, Burke had not less independence of character, and immeasurably more of the
milk of human kindness than Thomas Paine, and to
add that the happiness of the humblest was never
far from his thoughts. But there is perhaps enough
truth in them to suggest that, even to the broad
humanity and penetrating insight of Burke, the
wrongs and miseries of down-trodden subjects

lacked something of the reality and significance which they wore to the eye of one who, with all his bitterness and class-hatred, saw them from the inside.

Nor can the well-worn argument from the political ignorance of the multitude, which has always done duty at every proposed extension of the franchise, be any longer pressed. Even if it had force in the days when Burke set his face as a flint against all parliamentary reform, those days, if they have not already passed, are swiftly passing. Happily the opportunities for political knowledge can no longer be said to be the monopoly of any class in the State. The compulsory school, the newspaper, the cheapened press, the platform, the lecture, the organised effort of intellectual propagandism, the rise and progress of universities in great cities are rapidly bringing political knowledge within all but universal reach. And though *reach* is one thing and *grasp* another, and though obviously enough ignorance has not departed, nor indeed is ever likely to depart, it is beyond all question steadily ceasing to be the badge of any class— except the class of the ignorant in all classes.

It is, however, not on the score of political ignorance only that Burke would exclude the multitude. For, as we have seen, the quality that, in his scale of valuation, is above all others needful in affairs is not knowledge, indispensable though that may be, but practical wisdom. It is, in other words, what, on its more ordinary levels we call good sense, and what, as found in the statesman, Burke calls ' prudence,' and magnifies as the mother of all the political virtues. For this, and this alone, is the faculty which enables its possessor, not merely to know facts and apprehend principles, but to apply principles to facts in the thousand concrete decisions which have to be made by politicians in their actual contact with circumstances and conduct of affairs. And we know—for he has left us in no manner of doubt—where Burke believed this quality was to be found, and also where it was not to be found. It was to be found conspicuously in his ' natural aristocracy ' and, though in greatly diminished degree, in the close electorates that stood behind them : it was not to be found in those ' whose talk is of bullocks,' and suchlike. In the former his faith is firm ; in the latter he has no faith at all.

Nor is this attitude unreasonable. Practical wisdom, even in its more modest form of common sense, is not to be lightly reckoned upon in mankind at large. It is none too common. It is not the gift of nature, nor can it be got from books, nor imparted like knowledge in schools or lecture-rooms. It comes, mainly at any rate, through practice and the actual conduct of life. It is by making decisions, sometimes by making blunders, that the blunders come to be fewer and the decisions sounder; nor will wisdom ever emerge, not even when natural gifts and knowledge are present in abundance, unless there be experience to furnish the opportunities for its exercise and slowly won development. And should it happen, by the exigencies of a humble lot and a contracted life, that such opportunities are denied, it is in vain to look for 'prudence' there, except in the non-political form that suffices to deal with the small concerns of private life. This is what Burke undoubtedly felt. It is not necessary to place his estimate of men too low, by the supposition that he would have denied the existence of sagacity and common sense in the ordinary conduct of their private lives. But when it came to the larger affairs of politics, it was different. These were quite beyond the scope of the rank and file; beyond their experience, beyond their knowledge, beyond their judgment, beyond their competence. Hence their exclusion.

It is not for democracy to deny the strength of this position. It cannot deny that, if the opportunities for the development of any human faculty be absent, that faculty will never be found except in meagre and inadequate degree; and political faculty is no exception to this rule. On the contrary, the fullest and frankest recognition of this fact is precisely one of the points on which democracy must insist. It must insist upon it in order that it may go on to affirm that, under the conditions of our modern social life, these opportunities, which rightly count for so much, are no longer denied to those classes whom Burke excludes. For in the modern state, the preparation for participation in political life has come to be far wider than politics. That astonishing growth in social organisation which has signalised the nineteenth century, has covered the land with a vast network not only of private enterprises, but of societies, leagues, unions, combinations, clubs, whose name is legion. Many of them are, of course, not in the stricter sense political. They have not been organised for strictly political ends at all : their aims have been commercial, industrial, social. Yet none the less on that account, they fulfil a political function of the first importance, because they provide a school and training-ground of civic quality. Be it trades-union, benefit club, friendly society, co-operative enterprise, charitable association, or what not, and be they never so diverse in the ends or interests for which they stand, they are all alike in this : they lift their members out of a narrowing absorption in private life ; they familiarise them with public ends and the conduct of affairs on a large scale ; and they teach them, through actual experience, the value and the discipline of organised collective effort. And if we add to this that reiterated strides in parliamentary reform, with universal and com-

pulsory education as its ally, have opened the door
for participation in the many graded activities of
rural, municipal, and national politics, it is far from
Utopian to believe that, by the cumulative force of
all these influences, the rank and file of the democratic State must steadily advance, not only in
political information, but—a still greater gain—in
that capacity for affairs which in Burke's estimate,
and possibly enough in Burke's age, they so conspicuously lacked. This is that 'education in the
widest sense of the word' on which J. S. Mill so
rightly relied—the education of actual participation in organised social and political work. It is
the only finally efficient school of political good
sense and practical wisdom.

It does not follow from this, however, that democracy has little to learn from the teaching of Burke.
On two cardinal points at any rate, it carries a
message that is greatly needed : the one, his conception of a representative as different from a delegate ; the other, his plea for a 'natural aristocracy.' These are intimately connected, but we
may take them in turn.

(c) Representatives and Delegates

It is often supposed, and sometimes regarded as
inevitable, that in proportion as democracy runs
its course the representative must needs dwindle

into the delegate. Not unnaturally. It would be
a childish ignorance to place a democracy in power
and to fancy that it is not certain to use it. Only
innocence or folly would put a weapon into energetic hands without reckoning that it will certainly
be vigorously handled. And they live in a fool's
paradise who think, if there be any such, that a
democratic electorate will not be minded to take
its destinies into its own hands. Gladstone once
said—and significantly enough the words come in
a context in which he is pleading for the extension
of the franchise—that ' the people must be passive.'
He even said it was so ' written with a pen of iron
on the rock of human destiny.' [1]   But the passivity,
if that be the word for it, must be understood with
reservations. For it is of the essence of the democratic spirit and ideal to strive to make the whole
community, not only in the occasional crises of
elections but in the not less important intervals
between elections, politically alive in the lives of
all its citizens. Its claim to foster, more than any
other form of government, the organic unity which is
the prime condition of a nation's strength, depends,
as has been already urged,[2] upon its being content
with nothing less. Nor can there be a doubt that
this must vitally affect the relation of electorate and
representative. As matter of fact it has shattered
beyond recovery the Whig theory and practice of

[1] *Gleanings of Past Years*, vol. i.   [2] P. 226.

virtual representation, and insisted upon substituting actual representation. And democracy has done this not because it has, like Bentham and James Mill and the sectarian radicals who followed them, come to regard virtual representatives as plunderers of the public, but for the simpler and less corrosive reason that the representatives of a free people must be chosen, and expected to render an account of their stewardship to their constituents. The responsibility of the representative to the electorate is so fundamental to the democratic creed that no genuine believer in democracy can possibly abjure it; not even although he may cheerfully concede, what the utilitarians churlishly denied, that many a virtual representative might be a man of honour, probity, public spirit, and wisdom. He cannot abjure it for the obvious reason that, where democracy is real, it must assert its will in the directing of policy and in the management of affairs.

It is one thing, however, to insist that representatives must be chosen and held to their responsibility, and another thing to turn them into delegates. And it is here that Burke has his message. For none of all our publicists, as we have seen,[1] has more firmly and more passionately protested against the fallacy that under representative institutions the representative should be a delegate. He pro-

[1] P. 165.

tested against this even under the close and presumably select franchise of his day. Such faith in constituencies as he had, vanished from the moment when an electorate showed signs of presuming to degrade the member of their choice into the mouthpiece and agent of their instructions. Like Macaulay after him, he told his constituents to the face that he meant to serve them with his labour, his judgment, his convictions, or not at all ; and could even administer to them the doubtful consolation that he had ' maintained their interest against their opinions with a constancy that became him.' [1]

Such is his legacy. And to none is it so needful as to the large and mixed electorates of democracy triumphant. For it is not in parliaments of delegates, enslaved to constituencies, caucuses, and parties, and mortgaged in judgment, that the natural aristocracy of democracy is likely to be found. Burke goes to the quick, nor of all his pregnant utterances is there one that is truer, when he says that the lovers of freedom must themselves be free—free to speak and to act upon their judgment. For of all slaveries the most humiliating to any leader of men is the slavery of the judgment, which is also the subjection of the conscience ; and of all tyrannies the worst is the tyranny of an electorate which, exchanging confidence for distrust, would fain transform a man of intelligence, honour, and patriot-

[1] Speech at Bristol previous to the election in 1780.

ism into a conduit for instructions which he must execute to the letter, on penalty of being driven from political life. Democracy has long learnt to hate the tyrants whose subjects are slaves : it must learn with equal thoroughness to despise the elected slaves whose tyrants are subjects. It has come to repose its trust in the collective wisdom : it must come equally to realise that collective wisdom will never be wiser than in choosing leaders who can lead, and reposing a large discretion in their hands. For the fact is not to be evaded, being as it is inseparable from the intricacy, complexity, urgency, cross-currents, and baffling confusions of all great political problems, that there are many decisions, and not on matters of mere detail alone, of which large electorates, by reason of their size, their lack of time, their want of accurate knowledge, their divided counsels, their passions, are inherently incapable. Nor is it their delegates that will help them out—not so long as it remains the fact that no democracy ever was, or ever will be, *led* by delegates. It would be a contradiction in terms. For there are two things which democracy can never unite : *the one* is the leadership of a natural aristocracy based on democratic representative institutions —that leadership for which, by the very magnitude of its legitimate equalitarian ambitions, and the problems these have raised, it has intensified the need ; *the other* is the perversion of the just and in-

evitable democratic claim to choose its own leaders
and to shape the destinies of the nation, into the
distrust and dictation which sterilise the political
wisdom, the ' prudence,' which is the greatest gift
which leadership can bring to the service of a people.

Nor need there be apprehensions that, by devolving
a large discretion on its leaders, democracy will
either weaken its case, or find its occupation gone.
It will strengthen its case. For it is when democracy becomes delegative that it lies open to assault.
It is, in truth, the easiest of tasks for its assailants,
Lowe (Lord Sherbrooke) for example, or Sir Henry
Maine, first to insist that political problems are
so complex, so intricate, so baffling, that they are
enough to tax the wits of the wisest, as they certainly may ; and then to turn round and ask, with
many a flout and sarcasm, if questions such as these
are likely to be solved by the votes of a mob. But
this is not the question which representative democracy has to answer. It does not pin its faith to
vox populi vox dei and nothing more ; nor does
its appeal to polling-booth and ballot-box rest on a
blind faith that majorities, however overwhelming,
can solve any political problem whatever by mere
weight of votes. Its hopes must always centre,
and the case for it must always turn, upon the men
whom polling-booth and ballot-box send up to
grapple with problems at closer quarters, and more
searchingly, than is ever possible for even the most

enlightened of electorates. To express needs and
grievances, to organise political associations, to hold
public meetings, freely to discuss both measures and
men, vigilantly to watch administration, and, above
all, to pronounce a verdict on measures or policies
when these come before them in their broad issues
after having been well threshed out in press, platform, or parliament—these are the functions of the
electorate. Or rather they are part of its functions :
the other part is its choice of men—men whose task
it is to serve their constituents indeed, but to serve
them, as Burke served his, without sacrifice of
freedom, conscience, and independent judgment.
Grant that it is not an easy task. Just how far
a constituency may particularise its will ; just
when and where the member of its choice may
waive his personal judgment without compromising
his sincerity—these are matters incapable of exact
definition. No hard and fast lines can be laid down
for them which may not change with circumstances.
There will always be room for give and take on both
sides. The vital matter is that electorates, if only
for their own sake, should recognise that the man of
their choice is not fit to be chosen if he have not a
mind and will of his own ; and that a resolute refusal to multiply pledges is, as Burke truly taught,
one of the prime conditions of securing energetic
and disinterested service. Nor is it ever to be forgotten that, under any form of constitution, it is

not service only that is needed : it is the service that is also leadership. This, however, will be more evident when we have considered Burke's conception of a natural aristocracy.

(d) *The Need for a Natural Aristocracy*

For Burke's feet were never on surer ground than when, as we have seen,[1] he argued that a civil society, by the very conditions of social struggle and growth, must needs evolve ' a natural aristocracy, without which there is no nation.' For a natural aristocracy is neither a product of social artifice, nor a parasitical growth : it is the inevitable result of the long and gradual process whereby society passes from the looser groupings and cohesions of primitive ages on to the larger and more richly integrated forms of civilised organisation. There is a striking passage in which Bagehot the economist, when enlarging on what he calls the necessarily ' monarchical structure ' of the modern business world, puts this point with his wonted animation : ' This monarchical structure,' he proceeds, ' increases as society goes on, just as the corresponding structure of war business does, and from the same causes. In primitive times, a battle depended as much on the prowess of the best fighting men, of some Hector or some Achilles, as on the

[1] P. 173.

good science of the general. But nowadays it is
a man at the far end of a telegraph wire—a Count
Möltke with his head over some papers—who sees
that the proper persons are slain, and who secures
the victory. So in commerce. The primitive
weavers are separate men with looms apiece, the
primitive weapon-makers separate men with flints
apiece ; there is no organised action, no planning,
contriving, or foreseeing in either trade, except on
the smallest scale ; but now the whole is an affair
of money and management ; of a thinking man in
a dark office, computing the prices of guns or wor-
steds.' [1] If these words are true of war and industry,
they are not less true of politics. And they are
never truer than when the course of political evolution has given birth to the democratic state. Unfortunately this is often missed. Too often and too
easily it is assumed that democracy levels. And so,
in conspicuous ways, it does. It levels down the
superiorities of prerogative, privilege and monopoly : it levels up the inferiorities of social disadvantage and political disability. But it does not,
nor can it ever, equalise. If it deposes a hereditary
aristocracy, not to say an aristocracy of Whig
' trustees,' it is driven on, by the needs it itself
creates, to find a new aristocracy of its own. By the
very fervour and persistence of its passion for
equality it creates new inequalities in demolishing

[1] *Economic Studies*, p. 53.

old ones. And this result follows from three causes, so closely concatenated that they might be said to furnish a kind of logic of democratic politics.

The *first* of these is that the passion for equality—the ruling passion of democracy if De Tocqueville is to be believed—creates problems. And not political problems only, such as touch parliamentary reform and government, but a crowd of social problems which follow in the train of the demand for more equality of opportunity and less inequality of wealth. The *second* point is that these problems have come to be of such magnitude that it has now for some time been recognised that nothing short of organised collective effort, private and public, and the resources it can command, can hope to solve them. Hence that astonishing growth of organisations which has steadily increased in defiance of all pessimistic prophecies of social disintegration (those, for example, of Carlyle), till at the end of every vista we see a union, a federation, a league, a society, a syndicate, a commission, a conference, and what not. And the *third* consideration is that, where there are organisations, there, as never before, there are to be found the need and the opportunities of leadership. It is an illusion to suppose that social organisation, however democratic, abates, far less supersedes, the need for leaders. It intensifies it. For these practical problems, with which organised effort is needed to grapple, are admittedly of a most intricate and baffling complexity. Many a student of society has felt the need of a life-time for their investigation. And many a statesman must have felt that he would give much, if only it were possible to suspend decision and action till he had more adequately analysed and grasped the conditions with which he has to deal. Yet this is what he cannot do. The world, the democratic world at any rate, does not suffer him to do it. For the problems that face him are not only complex : they are urgent. The hungry spirit, the deep dissatisfactions, the equalitarian ambitions of democracy make them urgent, clamant. Suspense of judgment, that privilege of the student, is denied to the man of affairs who, all too often for his own peace of mind, finds himself compelled to move to his solutions by decisions which, to the eye of the student, must seem to verge perilously near a leap in the dark.

Hence the result, which brings us back again to the teaching of Burke, that the solution of all great political questions demands nothing less than the union of two qualities, both admirable, both indispensable, but extraordinarily difficult to unite : the searching, patient, analytic grasp of conditions, and the virile practical judgment, the ' prudence ' of Burke's panegyric, which knows when to cut deliberations short, to grasp the skirts of opportunity, and to decide resolutely what has here and now to

be done.   For it is the union of these two qualities
that is the passport to statesmanship.   Nothing
less will suffice.   The massive push of collective
effort is not enough.   The deliberations and resolutions of the collective wisdom of ordinary men,
however well intentioned and earnest, are not
enough.   Wherever political questions are great,
complex, baffling, urgent, they will inevitably, no
matter what the form of government may be, prove
themselves to be both the touchstone and the whet-
stone of leadership.   For organisations do not
work by a human automatism, nor are they self-
adjusting organisms such as political biologists
press upon us as analogies.   If they are to achieve
the tasks for which they are called into being, they
must be vitalised, directed, and controlled by the
proximate efficient forces of exceptionally gifted
and well-trained human wills.

This is what Burke saw so clearly and expressed
so loftily in his description of a ' natural aristocracy.'
He had thought much about equality.   He had
thought much about inequality.   And one of the
conclusions to which he had come was that those
who attempt to level can never equalise.   No; they
can never equalise, because by the inborn and ineffaceable inequalities of human faculty, by the laws
of social struggle and growth—the ' discipline of
nature,' as he called it—and by the nature of social
organisation, there must always emerge in every

civil society, and indeed in every serious enterprise which tests the stuff of which men are made, ' a natural aristocracy, without which there is no nation.'

Nor does it much impair the value of Burke's message here that his natural aristocracy is so manifestly aristocratic in the narrower as well as in the wider and more literal sense of the word. It was offered to the world as a plea for the Whig aristocracy of the eighteenth century by one who, from a lifelong knowledge of men and affairs, was convinced that the England of his day could produce such men ; and we must leave it to the historians to say how well, or how ill, the original corresponded to the picture. Nor need it be suggested that the tribute—the greatest surely ever paid to the Whigs —was undeserved. For the Whig leaders, be their limitations what they may, were above all things men of affairs. Yet Burke's delineation—perhaps we should call it his ideal—has a far wider and more lasting significance than as an apotheosis of Whig ascendency. It may serve as a reminder that the time has come when the feud between democracy and aristocracy (rightly so-called) should cease, and when radicalism itself, if it is to solve the problems which by its masterful equalitarian ambitions it has thrust to the front, must find, on its own terms, and by its own methods, a new natural aristocracy of its own. Nor would it befit even the most ardent radicalism, in the interest of the causes it has at heart, to brush Burke's roll of leadership [1] aside, or even wish a single class or category expunged. It would be better employed in making additions to it. For the vulnerability of Burke's conception lies not in what it includes, but in what by its silence it excludes ; and criticism must accordingly take the more sympathetic form of insisting that it needs to be broadened to suit the greatly altered requirements of a social system which has, perhaps irrevocably, and socially as well as politically, cast in its lot with democracy.

For it need hardly be said that since Burke died (1797) the whole social and political situation has been transformed. Industry and commerce have become so vast a system that they have called into being an endlessly diversified middle class whose vocation is the management of affairs. The ' rich traders ' who mark the lower limit of Burke's inclusions do not cover a tithe of them. And the same thing has happened, and seems likely to happen in accelerated degree, in the ranks of labour. For it is not the growth of labour in volume, though it is vast ; nor its advance in specialisation and mechanical skill that is the salient fact of political significance. It is that progress in organisation, so notable in our day, which has brought many a man, sprung from the ranks, to find himself swaying

[1] P. 175.

the policy and action of trade-unions and federations which number their members by millions. These are facts which no one can doubt. Some may view them with hope, some with alarm, some with despair ; but none may dispute that, by the steady pressure of economic and social forces even more than by the redistributions of political power, which these have again and again necessitated, the ranks of leadership have been recruited from quarters where Burke never dreamed of finding it. For the whole framework of society has changed so fundamentally that it would be a miracle if the scope for leadership had not changed and widened along with it. The excluded multitude, who were still to Burke but ' the objects of protection and the means of force,' have long ago been enlisted on the effective British public : the ' British public,' which on his computation were but 400,000 souls all told, has now for some time been swallowed up in democratic electorates : the close constituencies, with their handful of voters, with which he was so well content, have been enlarged beyond recognition. Is it wonderful if his ' natural aristocracy ' has been expanded likewise ?

This, however, as we have sufficiently seen, was precisely the line of change which Burke abhorred as pregnant with ruin. His belief in reform, on which he prided himself to the end of his days, deserted him on the moment when reform assumed the fatal aspect of organic, constitutional innovation. So much so, that amongst the many fears that haunted his later years we may search in vain for the fear, so transparent in the Whigs as well as in the Tories of 1832, that unbending conservative resistance might prove infinitely more disastrous than reforming democratic adventure. At times, indeed, this seems to have crossed his mind : we have seen him invoking the very principle on which Macaulay justifies the concessions of 1832—the far-reaching principle that, if the constitution does not destroy exclusions, exclusions will destroy the constitution. But it was clearly not a principle which he was himself prepared to universalise. It would be truer to say of him that his faith in the constitution, a faith so strong and confident, that he is ready at times to take his stand upon it and to defy radicalism to do its worst, is, nevertheless, not strong and confident enough. Faith in the constitution, as it stands —yes, and all too much of it. But not faith enough that a constitution may, and indeed must, live and thrive upon those very constitutional reforms which change its structure. And this is the more striking because there is so much in his thought that might seem to point towards this perception. Did he not say that ' nothing can rest on its original plan ? ' Did he not admit that change may be ' a principle of conservation ' ? Did he not declare that to preserve old establishments when the reason for them is gone is no better than to burn precious incense in the tombs, and to offer meat and drink to the dead ? Did he not himself in his day press for reforms ? He had no doubt that the English people would be strengthened by these reforms. Yet he could not believe that the constitution could be similarly strengthened. For to the many excellences which move him to rhapsodies of panegyric he could not find it in him to add the excellence, than which there is none greater, that a constitution may have the vitality that emerges from the reformers' hands with a stronger life than ever. Surely it is of the essence of life in all its modes that it victoriously persists and develops through many changes which may profoundly modify it both in structure and in functions. It is a truism in biology : it ought to be a truism in politics.

To this line of criticism Burke undoubtedly lays himself open. He does this all the more because he is never to be classed with the pedants who lose sight of spirit in the worship of letter. On the contrary no political thinker whatsoever has had a clearer perception that a constitution is alive. ' Do not dream,' he says, ' that your letters of office, and your instructions, and your suspending clauses, are the things that hold together the great contexture of this mysterious whole. These things do not make your government. Dead instruments, passive tools as they are, it is the spirit of the English communion that gives all their life and efficacy to them. It is the spirit of the English constitution, which, infused through the mighty mass, pervades, feeds, unites, invigorates, vivifies, every part of the Empire, even down to the minutest member.' [1]   Nothing can be truer. But it hardly bespeaks much faith in this spirit of the constitution to deny, as in effect Burke passionately denies, that it might clothe itself in a better and less contracted form than the Old Whig constitution of the eighteenth century.

(e) *The Limitations of Burke's Political Ideal*

Nor is it easy to believe that, even for purposes of defence, this inflexible conservatism was the best resource against those radical and, as he thought, revolutionary ideals which it was the peculiar mission of his later years to deride and demolish. When a statesman finds himself face to face with ideals he detests, it is never enough to meet them by criticism and invective. Even when ideals may be false and fanatical, they will seldom, if they have once found lodgment in the popular mind, be driven from the field till they are met by some rival ideal strong and attractive enough to oust them from their tenancy. The forward-struggling spirit of man, especially of masses of men chafing under obstructions, is not to be won by negations. So long as reason and imagina-

---

[1] Speech on Conciliation with America.

tion keep their hold on life, mankind will cleave to
whatever plan or project seems to satisfy that
craving for betterment which lies deep in, at any
rate, all Western peoples. Hence the familiar remark—it is what Maine said of the ' broken-down
theories ' of Bentham and Rousseau—that ideals
may survive long after their brains are out. They
do survive, and they will continue to survive, if
there be no counter-ideal to supersede them.

It is here that Burke is lacking. One may not
say that he has no ideal to offer ; and indeed it has
been said a hundred times that the constitution he
worshipped was not the constitution as it was, but
a glorified picture of it as it shaped itself in his
soaring imagination. Nor is the reader to be envied
who can rise from his pages without having found
an ideal. But it is an ideal that has the defects of
its qualities. For, when all is said, the political
imagination of Burke spent its marvellous force
almost wholly in two directions. In the one direction it conjured up with the vividness of actual
vision the disasters which radical reforms, so easy to
initiate, and so hard to control, might carry in their
train : in the other it lavished its powers in glori-
fying the present as a legacy of priceless practical
value inherited from the ever-memorable past. The
result is splendid, and it is an incomparably richer
thing than the ideals of Rousseau or Paine or Price
or Godwin. But it has limitations which these

escaped. As a gospel for his age, or for any age, it has the fatal defect that, in its rooted distrust of theories and theorists, it finds hardly any place for political ideals as serious attempts to forefigure the destinies of a people as not less Divinely willed than its eventful past history or present achievement. And, by consequence, it fails to touch the future with the reformer's hope and conviction of better days to come.

> ' The echoes of the past within his brain,
> The sunrise of the future on his face,'

—they are both the attributes of all great states-manship. But if the sunrise of the future ever irradiates the pages of Burke, it is all too quickly to be quenched, at best in the clouds that veil the incalculable future, and at worst in the incendiary smoke of revolutionary fires. It is this that leaves our gratitude not unmixed with regrets. For Burke is no ordinary statesman, from whom it is enough to expect, that, if he look beyond the present at all, he should see no further than the next practical step in advance. Nor is he to be judged as such. It would do him wrong being so majestical. He is a political genius of the first order ; and just because he is so great it is impossible to withhold from him the tribute of wishing for more than he has actually given. No one had it in him as he had to give his country a comprehensive and satisfying political ideal. He had the knowledge, the imagination,

the experience ; and, not least, he had the religious
faith which, when it strikes alliance with the idealis-
ing spirit, makes all the difference between ideals
that are but subjective dreams and ideals which are
beliefs that nerve to action. Nor is the reader who
has felt the power and fascination of his pages to be
blamed if he falls to wondering how much of the
strife and embitterment of the nineteenth century
might have been averted, if this master in politics
had given the reins to his imagination as freely and
sympathetically in looking forward to posterity as
in looking backward to ancestors. But it was not
in that path he was to walk. Somehow, though not,
as we have seen, without reasons, his faith failed him.
It was strong enough to make the course of history
divine, to consecrate the legacy of the past, to
intensify the significance and the responsibilities
of the present. But it could not inspire an ideal
of constitutional and social progress. ' Perhaps,'
he once remarked, with even more than his wonted
distrust of thought divorced from actuality, ' the
only moral trust with any certainty in our hands is
the care of our own time.' [1]

The result is that we find in Burke's writings the
presence of two things, and the absence of a third.
We find an unfaltering faith in the presence of a
' Divine tactic ' in the lives of men and nations.
We find also an *apologia* such as has never been

[1] *Appeal.*

equalled, for the existing social and political system as it has come to be by the long toil of successive generations. What we do not find, and are fain to wish for, and most of all from a thinker to whom the happiness of the people was always paramount, is some encouragement for the hope that the ' stupendous Wisdom ' which has done so much in the past, and even till now, will not fail to operate in the varieties of untried being through which the State, even the democratic State, must pass in the vicissitudes and adventures of the future.